GUARDIANS
of the
SEAS

'This book is an invaluable first-hand account of the intrepid carrier-based Indian naval operations in the Bay of Bengal, which resulted in the successful conclusion of India's war against Pakistan in 1971. Rear Admiral S.K. Gupta as fighter pilot and Commodore Gurnam Singh as air engineer are true masters of their specializations.'

Vice Admiral H. Johnson, PVSM, VSM (Retd)
Former Flag Officer Commanding-in Chief,
Western Naval Command, Mumbai

'The book exceptionally describes the preparation, maintenance, operational details and post sortie maintenance to ensure that the squadron maintained 100 per cent serviceability of Sea Hawk fighters on board INS *Vikrant*. The authors have also injected a sense of commitment and laborious effort of the technical crew and the pilots.'

Vice Admiral Shekhar Sinha
PVSM, AVSM, NM & Bar and ADC (Retd)
Former Commander-in-Chief, Western Naval Command,
Chief of Integrated Defence Staff,
Chairman, Board of Trustees, India Foundation

'*Guardians of the Seas* is a gripping account of the 1971 war, which gave the Indian Navy its finest hour. A work that will interest the scholar and layperson alike, it is a rich addition to the slim inventory of books on the Indian Navy.'

Commodore Srikant B. Kesnur, VSM (Retd), PhD
Author and Navy Historian

'The authors' first-hand, lucid account of the 1971 Indo-Pak War together with the various activities prior and during the war makes for an engaging read. The narrative weaves with ease, successful integration and coordination at different levels.'

Commodore Lalit Shanker (Retd)
Ex-Commander, INS *Vikrant*

GUARDIANS
of the
SEAS

TRIUMPH OF THE INDIAN NAVY AND ITS AIR POWER IN THE 1971 WAR

Rear Admiral S.K. Gupta *and*
Commodore Gurnam Singh

RUPA

Published by
Rupa Publications India Pvt. Ltd 2023
7/16, Ansari Road, Daryaganj
New Delhi 110002

Sales centres:
Bengaluru Chennai
Hyderabad Jaipur Kathmandu
Kolkata Mumbai Prayagraj

P-ISBN: 978-93-5702-770-0
E-ISBN: 978-93-5702-908-7

First impression 2023

10 9 8 7 6 5 4 3 2 1

The moral right of the authors has been asserted.

Printed in India

जलमेवयस्य, बलमेवतस्य

(He who rules over the seas is all powerful)

This book is dedicated to the pioneers of naval aviation who laid the foundation of India's victory in the 1971 Indo-Pak War through their dedicated work, starting from India's independence, across the decades of 1950s and 1960s. We are forever indebted to them.

Contents

Foreword

I feel privileged to write the foreword to this book for two reasons. Firstly, I have known both the authors for many years. Rear Admiral S.K. Gupta (Retd) was commanding Indian Naval Air Squadron (INAS) 551, when I joined the unit as a 'rookie' naval aviator in 1968; and Commodore Gurnam Singh (Retd) was deputy of the Sea Harrier project team in the United Kingdom (UK), where we raised the new squadron in 1982–83. Secondly, both were active participants in the 1971 Bangladesh Liberation War, wherein they were decorated for conspicuous gallantry. There could not be a duo, better qualified to write a book such as this.

Throughout India's ancient history, a succession of Central Asian invaders descended from the passes of the Hindu Kush to plunder the rich Indo-Gangetic Plain. However, the late fifteenth century saw the beginning of incursions over the shores of Peninsular India by Europeans. Those who had come by land stayed on and were assimilated into India's rich cultural fabric, but those who had arrived by sea routes came only to exploit India, to enslave its people and to take home its riches. The lesson that must remain etched in Indian minds is this: Weakness at sea cost India its freedom, impoverished the nation, and set back the industrial, economic and social progress by a century or more.

There is a profound irony here because India has a rich and ancient maritime tradition, which had inspired seafaring enterprises for centuries, both on its western and eastern seaboards. However, by the early eleventh century, Indian maritime power went into rapid decline, and oceanic trade in the Indian seas passed into the hands of the Arabs. Then followed two centuries of European dominance of the East, exercised through sea power.

The onset of Independence, regrettably, did little to banish the inherited Indian affliction of 'sea-blindness'. The fledgling Indian Navy remained a 'Cinderella' service, surviving from one shoestring budget to the next. Fortuitously, the 1971 war provided an opportunity for the navy's bold leadership to demonstrate its prowess. This war saw the Service employing the full gamut of its maritime capabilities, including aircraft carrier operations, missile warfare, submarine and anti-submarine operations, and trade warfare. Indian Navy's sterling contribution to this successful tri-service campaign demonstrated the navy's potential as a powerful instrument of state policy.

The account that you are about to read is a passionate appeal by the authors to their countrymen, prompting them about India's past neglect of maritime security and its vital relevance for the country's future. At the macro-level, they remind us about the historical omissions that led to India's 200-year-long colonization by Britain, the origin and growth of the Indian Navy and the genesis of its aviation arm. At the micro-level, they lead the reader through fascinating minutiae about the acquisition of India's first aircraft carrier, INS *Vikrant*, the selection of its aircraft and the training of pioneering carrier pilots and technical crew.

The delectable core of the book lies in the detailed narrative of the navy's preparation for impending hostilities and personal accounts of the day-to-day conduct of operations during the 1971 war, on board INS *Vikrant*. The cutting edge of the navy's air campaign against enemy targets in East Pakistan was formed by INAS 300, which gave an excellent account of itself under the command of Lt Cdr S.K. Gupta. For his outstanding gallantry and leadership in combat, the Squadron Commander was awarded the Maha Vir Chakra (MVC).

The squadron went into action with 18 Sea Hawk

fighter-bombers, and while attacking heavily defended targets, many of them returned with severe damages. The maintenance crew, led by the squadron's Air Engineer Officer (AEO), Lt Gurnam Singh, demonstrated skill, dedication and ingenuity of the highest order in working round the clock to repair each aircraft and send it back into action. The squadron ended its campaign with all 18 Sea Hawks in 'serviceable' state. For his outstanding leadership in combat, Lt Gurnam Singh was awarded the Nao Sena Medal (Gallantry).

Given their vital role in the conduct of *Vikrant's* air campaign, the main focus of the two authors has remained on naval operations off East Pakistan in the Bay of Bengal. They have also provided glimpses of important events of the 1971 maritime campaign, off West Pakistan and in the Arabian Sea.

This volume is a fascinating story of gallantry and dedication in war, and I have no doubt that it will find readership and appreciation—not just amongst the naval and military fraternities but also amongst the civilian community of historians and analysts, as well as the youth and laypersons.

—**Admiral Arun Prakash**
PVSM, AVSM, VrC, VSM (Retd)
Former Chief of Naval Staff
Dabolim, Goa

Authors' Note

I was a young lieutenant when the Indo-Pak War broke out in December 1971. It was a well-fought war and India won it decisively. A part of the story of that war, primarily from the naval aviation point of view, is told in this book. A question may be asked why now, half a century later? The answer lies in time. A lapse of half a century may be regarded sufficient to provide reasonable perspective for an event of this nature, magnitude and national significance.

We, the authors, are of the view that the Indian victory in the 1971 war was unique. It was the first war fought by a sovereign India in nearly two millennia and won for the entire world to see. Ever since the reign of Ashoka the Great ended with his death in 232 BCE, the Indian subcontinent had been in turmoil. The invasion of India by Muhammad bin Qasim in 712 CE was followed by that of Mahmud of Ghazni in 1025. Muhammad Ghori defeated Prithviraj Chauhan in 1192 and established Muslim rule which, in one form or the other, continued till the fall of the last Mughal emperor in 1857, when the British took over the country and colonized it. India became free in 1947, with the partition of the country, leading to carving out of Pakistan. India declared itself a republic in 1950.

Free and sovereign India fought wars with Pakistan in 1947–48, 1965 and in 1971. Out of these, the first two ended in stalemate but the third one was a decisive victory for India. The war ended with Pakistan's defeat and surrender to India.

I was a young officer in 1971 and took part in the war—in the Bay of Bengal in the eastern theatre of the war—from the flight deck of INS *Vikrant* as the AEO of the celebrated INAS 300, which comprised Sea Hawk jet fighters. I had joined the squadron at Madras (now Chennai) in July 1971 and was on board INS *Vikrant* from July to November-end, preparing for a war that seemed imminent. The war broke out on 3–4 December 1971 and I participated in its conduct from INS *Vikrant* as part of the White Tigers Sea Hawk squadron.

To my mind, it was essential that the nation studies and understands how we had achieved the integration of the political leadership, army, navy, air force, para-military, citizens and bureaucracy, and welded them into a focussed and potent war machine. It was this instrument that wielded synchronized, heavy and powerful blows on Pakistan in the eastern and the western theatres, simultaneously, starting from the night of 3–4 December 1971. To the surprise and discomfiture of Pakistan, despite its bravado and powerful international friends, its armed forces crumbled in 13 days and the country was on its knees. Half of Pakistan broke away to form a new country, Bangladesh.

In the decades that followed 1971, one thought returned to me time and again. It had assumed the form of a question in my mind: 'How did we win the 1971 war? What did we do right?' I could not grasp the entire gamut of the war at the national level, but I felt that we could certainly attempt to do so for the Indian Navy or for that matter, for the Indian naval aviation. The idea behind this thought was that if we understand how we won in 1971—the preparation for war and its implementation—then the algorithm would help us the next time as well, whenever needed.

In this book, this consideration runs as an undercurrent, and an attempt has been made to analyse some factors that are relevant in this regard.

We believe that the 1971 war awakened India to the importance of acquiring capability and wherewithal of sea control, to be able to exercise effective control of the Indian Ocean, that too in the changing geopolitical scene in the Indo-Pacific region. These factors are essential for India to safeguard its maritime and strategic interests. We believe that as a legacy of the 1971 war, India has understood the need for a powerful navy for its own security as well as national interest. This conviction is behind the national effort to equip the Indian Navy with the state-of-the-art ships, aircraft carriers, submarines, aircraft, weapons, communication, infrastructure and human resources as India assumes its destined role in the international arena.

We thank Admiral Arun Prakash, former chief of the naval staff (CNS), for graciously accepting our request to pen a foreword to the book. He needs no introduction, as his name is known nationally as well as internationally as a first-grade carrier-borne fighter pilot of Sea Hawks; as the senior officer who introduced Sea Harrier, a vertical and/or short take-off and landing (V/STOL) aircraft in the Indian Navy; and a writer on the strategic and defence interests of India, with special focus on the Indian Navy and our role in the Indian Ocean and Indo-Pacific region.

It would be of interest to the readers to know that all three— Admiral Arun Prakash, Rear Admiral S.K. Gupta and I—played a key role in introduction of Sea Harriers in the Indian Navy. All three of us were holding appointments in London when the first batch of Indian Navy Sea Harriers were being built at British Aerospace, commissioned as a squadron at Royal Naval Air Station (RNAS) Yeovilton, and trained with the Royal Navy in 1981–85.

Both Rear Admiral S.K. Gupta and I were at the scene, on board INS *Vikrant*, from July 1971–December 1971, when the war finally ended. You will find first-hand descriptions and narrations of those days from the two of us in this book. Those were the times when history was being written. Also included in the book are the first-hand accounts of several officers who made their contribution to the war. There is also one senior sailor who survived the tragic sinking of INS *Khukri* in the Arabian Sea on the night of 9 December 1971. There are many more who played equally significant roles in the war, but the constraints of the book size have stayed our hand in including all such accounts. We apologize for that.

While researching this book and later putting it together, we needed to contact many people to clarify some aspects or verify some facts from the *Vikrant* years and the war days. The response was always most gratifying and humbling. We thank them profusely.

We also thank Yamini Chowdhury of Rupa Publications for publishing this book. We are also thankful to Veena Batra, Aurodeep Mukherji and Sakschi Verma for their meticulous editing. With their painstaking efforts, the book has assumed a presentable form for the readers.

—Commodore Gurnam Singh, NM (G) (Retd)
New Delhi

∾

Since July 1970, it appeared inconceivable that INS *Vikrant* could participate in any war, given its poor physical state, with one boiler restricting her speed to 14 knots. In a war, she could be an attractive target for an enemy's lurking submarine; and even if the air squadrons embarked on the aircraft carrier, they would be unable to operate from her deck with full fuel and weapon load. A wind speed of 24.5 knots over the flight deck was necessary for the launch and recovery of her Sea Hawk fighter aircraft. There were other problems too.

The lack of essential spares led to poor availability of Sea Hawks; their age increased their defect rate and availability for flying. The squadron also lacked experienced deck-qualified pilots when war clouds were gathering, and war with Pakistan was imminent. This was the situation in July 1971, when INS

Vikrant sailed out from Bombay (now Mumbai) to the east coast for Madras to keep herself relatively safe from the enemy. It is to the credit of the then CNS, Admiral S.M. Nanda, who convinced key planners on his staff, that even given these conditions, INS *Vikrant* with her two air squadrons must be made operational for war in four months, even if it meant the ship had to operate at lower speed.

The Commanding Officer of INS Vikrant, Captain Swaraj Parkash (later vice admiral), with his chosen heads of the air and engineering departments, gallantly took up the challenge. INS *Vikrant* succeeded in participating in the war by blockading the approaches and exits to and from erstwhile East Pakistan, whilst her aircraft attacked shipping and shore targets, preventing both escape and interference from an outside power. It is also worth mentioning that in the war, which lasted just 13 days, Sea Hawks were not able to fly for three days owing to insufficient natural wind, which when added to the ship's speed should have given the magic figure of 24.5 knots or more, facilitating the operation of Sea Hawk fighter jets from the deck of *Vikrant*.

At the commencement of hostilities in the western sector, the Indian Navy carried out bold and daring attacks on Karachi port by the newly-inducted missile boats that were highly successful in targeting warships and other shipping at the port. Thereafter, Pakistan Navy was unable to stir out of Karachi. With INS *Vikrant* in the Bay of Bengal, it was appreciated that danger at sea lay only from Pakistan submarine PNS Ghazi, which was their only submarine that had the endurance to operate in the Bay of Bengal. Hence, the aircraft carrier's movements were a guarded secret ever since she was sailed out from harm's way to the east coast. This was just as well, as Ghazi was always unsure of the carrier's position, and instead met its own doom outside Vizag port!

It was not until mid-October 1971 that the Sea Hawks' availability improved with the supply of aircraft spares and the effort of the squadron's engineers. Around the same time, the more experienced pilots who had served on the carrier earlier joined the squadron. Soon, there were adequate Sea Hawks and pilots to operate from the carrier. In just 24 flying days in four months, with 15 pilots embarked from August to November, INS *Vikrant* became fully operational with her squadrons. By early November, the carrier personnel with the squadron crews were raring to go!

On declaration of war on the night of 3 December, successive air strikes launched from INS *Vikrant* next morning wreaked havoc on the enemy by destroying or neutralizing their ships, and attacking designated and opportune targets in Cox's Bazar, Chittagong, Dohazari, Khulna, Changla and Mongla. No ships could break the blockade and no aircraft could pass unchallenged. The Indian fleet ruled the seas around the northern Bay of Bengal. With the Indian Army fast closing in and the Indian Air Force (IAF) assuming complete air superiority over the war zone, the Indian Navy closed all supply and escape routes seawards.

There was no alternative for Pakistan other than to surrender and avoid further annihilation. The surrender by Pakistan with 93,000 troops, which was achieved after 13 days of war, saw the birth of a new nation, Bangladesh. This victory was a historical achievement for India, as the war ended before any interference was possible from the US Navy task force led by their super aircraft carrier *Enterprise*, which had cruised through the Strait of Malacca, arriving in the Andaman Sea.

The outcome of this war was that it weakened Pakistan and gave India supremacy in the Bay of Bengal region. It enhanced the prestige of our armed forces. Repatriation of the 93,000 prisoners of war (POW)—who had been treated humanely—back to the country that was defeated so decisively further enhanced India's prestige. It opened up trade relations between India and the new and friendly country, Bangladesh.

The effective 'out of the box' role played by our navy changed the mindset of our population and the planners in the direction of greater importance being given to our navy. The traditional defensive role of the navy was earlier confined to protecting our sea lanes, facilitating our commerce and defending our ports. An aggressive role was now added: one of ruling the seas around the subcontinent. It was a big step towards attaining the mantle of a regional power that could 'seal' the approaches to the Indian Ocean at Strait of Malacca in the East, and similarly carry out surveillance at the focal point around the Cape and along the African east coast to the Red Sea and Persian Gulf.

The significance of the proactive role played with great finesse by the Indian Navy during the 1971 war cannot be underestimated. The balanced growth of the force is already being witnessed in the years since.

—Rear Admiral Santosh Kumar Gupta
Maha Vir Chakra, NM (Retd)

Introduction
1971: A Year to Remember

The year 1971 was highly significant for India. It was the year when India waged a war against a foreign country and won it for the first time in its history since the invasion by Alexander in 326 BCE. This milestone came after the ones of 1947, when India gained independence from British colonial rule, and the year 1950, when 'We, the People of India' gave ourselves a Constitution and declared the nation a Sovereign Democratic Republic.

Before British colonization, India was a rich country enjoying 27 per cent share in the world economy. When the British left in 1947, India's share shrunk to a mere 3 per cent of the global gross domestic product (GDP).[1] The colonization of India by the British-authorized East India Company, from 1757 till 1857, and thereafter by the British Crown, damaged India severely. The consequences of these two centuries were such that, in 1947, India inherited from the British a broken economy—devastated from two centuries of loot and plunder driven by the profiteering and greed of the colonizer, imperial Britain. India had been reduced to penury.

Other than the systematic looting, the British also divided the country into two when departing from the Indian subcontinent. The areas in Punjab and Bengal wherein Muslims were in majority

[1] Tharoor, Shashi, *An Era of Darkness: The British Empire in India*, Aleph, 2016, p. 4.

were separated and made into a new country and given the name of Pakistan.

Not only did the British rule over the nation for 200 years, they also systematically subjugated the Indian people during that time. All important posts in the civil and military administration were held by white men, with Indians only involved in menial labour, being given junior posts in the administration. This denied Indians any opportunity of gaining hands-on experience in middle and higher levels of administration and governance. In 1857, F.J. Shore, the colonial administrator in Bengal, testified before the House of Commons to the effect that, in India, Indians had been 'excluded from every honour, dignity or office which the lowest Englishman could be prevailed upon to accept'[2]. The American writer, historian and philosopher Will Durant was aghast at the horrors of colonial rule in India and described the British colonization of India as one of 'political exclusion and social scorn'.[3]

As a result, when Indians were handed over the reins of the country in 1947, they had little or no real experience in running and governing a country the size of a subcontinent with a population of about 340 million.

The British had exploited the land mercilessly, and like everything else, had left Indian agriculture in ruins. The godowns and silos of the nation were running empty. There was widespread hunger, malnutrition, disease and low life expectancy. The Indians serving in the bureaucracy, defence and security forces were motivated to do their best, but they and the institutions they served were woefully inadequate in ability, expertise, capacity, numbers and funds. India needed huge investments in capital and infrastructural outlays, but the resources were scarce. This state also affected the armed forces.

However, the young nation took up the challenge of rebuilding

---

[2]Ibid. 60.
[3]Durant, Will, *A Case for India*, Strand Book Stall, Mumbai, 2007, p. 18.

everything from scratch. Through the tireless efforts of the government and civilians, India made progress, sometimes slow, sometimes in leaps and bounds. By 1971, India had made some progress towards understanding and improving the economy from the profound and devastating damage done over the previous two centuries of colonization. The food crisis was successfully addressed, and the crushing poverty from the time of Independence was alleviated to a great extent. There was progress in building up the army, air force and the navy by this time, which would turn out to be crucial that year.

Friction with Pakistan: The War of 1971

One of the most deeply problematic legacy of the British Empire in India was Partition. Separating the people of Punjab and Bengal on the basis of religion, as well as the horrors of Partition itself, resulted in deep scars. Ever since, for one reason or the other, the relations between Pakistan and India have not been cordial and peaceful. The two countries have had conflicts and skirmishes, and on at least four occasions, these have precipitated into open armed conflicts and wars.

The first was the invasion of the state of Jammu and Kashmir (J&K) by Pakistani tribesmen in October 1947. The second was the Indo-Pak War of 1965 when Pakistan invaded India in the western sector. The third was the Bangladesh Liberation War of 1971, and the last was the Kargil War of 1999. Of these, the first two ended in stalemates, with both sides claiming victory. Of the remaining two, India was able to prevail and take back the Indian areas encroached upon by Pakistan in the mountainous region of Kargil and force the Pakistani forces to withdraw after making Pakistan suffer heavy losses of men and material. The United States of America (USA) interceded on behalf of Pakistan to bring about a ceasefire.

Of the conflicts and wars fought between India and Pakistan since 1947, the Indo-Pak War of 1971 stands in a class of its own since it resulted in the most decisive and spectacular victory for India. The war was a result of India stepping in to free the people of erstwhile East Pakistan from the tyranny of West Pakistan, resulting in the creation of the free nation, Bangladesh. Within the brief span of two weeks, the Indian armed forces defeated Pakistan. Unlike on earlier occasions, this time, the Indian Navy did exceedingly well too. Naval attacks on Karachi; bottling up of most of the Pakistani fleet of warships within the bounds of Karachi harbour; disruption of the Pakistani trade and the commerce from its financial and commercial capital Karachi; the cutting of the maritime link between East and West Pakistan; attrition of Pakistani forces; and the contraband control in the Arabian Sea and in the Bay of Bengal, strangulated Pakistan and were instrumental in the quick capitulation of the Pakistani armed forces.

In the western theatre of the Arabian Sea, the Indian Navy carried out two missile attacks on the Karachi harbour, taking Pakistan's commercial capital and headquarters of the Pakistan Navy by total surprise. Many Pakistani naval ships and harbour installations were destroyed or severely damaged during these attacks. All foreign vessels were given notice to clear from the war zone promulgated by India. Some of them were also suspected to carry arms and ammunitions for the Pakistani armed forces or carry Pakistani troops. Therefore, they were targeted by the Indian armed forces as legitimate targets. Two merchant ships, the Liberian *Venus Challenger* of 10,065 tons and the Panamian *Gulf Star* of 1,280 tons, sank. British merchant ship *Harmattan* of 10,411 tons was damaged. The bulk oil storage installations were set on fire by the Indian attacks and burned for days. The orange flames of the conflagration rose to the sky. They rendered the Karachi sky bright red, and the orange glow from the conflagration could be seen from scores of miles away over the horizon, as reported by ships at sea. After this attack, the

Pakistan Navy did not leave the Karachi harbour during the rest of the war. Then on, the shipping routes leading to Karachi were under total control of Indian Navy, so much so that the foreign shipping lines began to take permission from the Indian Navy when they wanted to enter or leave Karachi harbour.

The Indian Navy, with its carrier battle group led by INS *Vikrant*, laid a total sea and air blockade in the Bay of Bengal for East Pakistan. Nothing could enter East Pakistan by air or by sea, or leave it from the direction of the Bay of Bengal. After blockading East Pakistan and isolating it completely from West Pakistan, the Sea Hawk jet fighters and the Alizé anti-submarine war planes, taking off from INS *Vikrant*, attacked the ports, ships, airports, runways, air traffic control towers, gunboats, electricity power plants, oil and ammunition dumps, and other strategic assets of East Pakistan relentlessly, by bombing, rocketing and strafing with aircraft mounted guns. They repeatedly attacked Dacca (now Dhaka), Chittagong, Mongla, Chalna, Khulna and other strategically important ports and targets in East Pakistan.

East Pakistan suffered the punishment meted out by the Indian Navy from the Bay of Bengal for two weeks and then broke down—it accepted defeat and surrendered. The contraband control and blockade measures put in place by the Indian Navy in the Bay of Bengal proved to be devastatingly crippling and effective. Seven merchant ships owned or chartered by Pakistani shipping agencies were captured at sea as 'prize' as per the recognized international naval practices and traditions of sea warfare. Three neutral ships carrying contraband were intercepted and taken to Indian ports, where they were held in detention. Twenty other neutral ships were either intercepted at sea or detained in Indian harbours on the commencement of hostilities. They were released later after offloading the contraband found on them.

The war ended with Pakistan losing half of its country, and the birth of a new free nation, Bangladesh. Pakistan accepted defeat and 93,000 officers and men of the Pakistani armed forces laid down their arms and surrendered to the Indian armed forces. Those present from India were high-ranking officers of the Indian armed forces and dignitaries, representing the Indian paramilitary forces and organizations that had taken part in the operations.

The surrender ceremony took place on 16 December 1971 at the Ramna Race Course in Dacca, which was then the capital of East Pakistan, and is now the capital of Bangladesh. It was an open public function in full glare of the Indian and the international media and watched by the whole world. The residents of Dacca came out in great numbers to witness the event.

Among the Pakistani officers and men who surrendered were Rear Admiral Mohammad Shariff, Commander of the Pakistani Eastern Naval Command, and Air Vice Marshal Patrick D. Callaghan of the Pakistan Eastern Air Force Command. The Instrument of Surrender was signed by Lt Gen. Amir Abdullah Khan Niazi and Lt Gen. Jagjit Singh Aurora in the presence of a large crowd of Bangladeshis and foreign media personnel. Lt Gen. Niazi removed his lanyard and handed over his pistol to Lt Gen. Aurora as a token of surrender. The crowd of the liberated Bangladeshi people on the race course erupted in celebration.

Consequences of the War

It is entirely possible that India might have to face unavoidable war or conflict in future. However, it can be said with reasonable conviction that for India, there would not be another result as decisive and consequential as the 1971 war. The way India welded itself into a potent fighting force and annihilated Pakistan was nothing short of a miracle. This is especially remarkable given the situation of the economy at the time.

It would be fair to suggest that the results of the 1971 Indo-Pak War went beyond the expectations of both India and Pakistan. When the war was declared in the first week of December 1971, it was perhaps not anticipated that Pakistan would capitulate and surrender so abjectly and completely, and that too in just two weeks' time. The international community also did not foresee that India would dismember Pakistan and break it into two, creating a new country out of it. As for Pakistan, it surely did not see itself coming out of the war with the humiliating loss of half its territory, the land and people of East Pakistan.

India, in fact, ought to analyse the events of 1971 to determine the factors that went right and ensured a near-perfect resonance among all the forces deployed in this war. These should be studied to understand how all the Indian forces at macro and micro levels got integrated to pack a powerful punch that broke Pakistan.

There is evidence in the public domain that lessons have been learnt. In the half century that has passed since December 1971, there have been changes in the interrelationship of the Indian Army, Indian Navy and the IAF, which are discernible. The most important has been the creation of the inter-services strategic command, the chief of defence staff (CDS). The CDS, by nature of his appointment, would help consolidate the inter-services analysis of the 1971 war while taking into account the geopolitical power shifts taking place in Asia Pacific region.

Mastery of the Seas

A major learning for India in 1971 was discovery of the power of sea control and domination. Although ruled by Britain for two centuries, India did not grasp that Britain could rule India, a country 10 times its size and 30 times larger in population, only because of its mastery of the seas. The simple truth that the mastery of the seas is fundamental for a country to wield power and influence in the world order was neither appreciated nor did it register in the Indian psyche. Indians also missed the developments in international warfare. After the Second World War, the naval aviation and the submarines had integrated with the traditional surface navy in Western countries, making it truly three-dimensional. As an instrument of power projection over long distances at sea, naval aviation was a force multiplier. But these developments had not made their appearance in the Indian Navy. The share of assets of ships and craft that the Indian Navy inherited from the British in 1947 was no better than the impoverished state of the country. This was the sorry state of the Indian Navy at the time of India's independence.

The sea connects all lands. A maritime power with unchallenged control of the seas can reach anywhere on the globe, unlike the traditional land-based army and the air force. The traditional large warships (a moving airfield in the form of an aircraft carrier with its jet fighter aircraft squadrons) brought the advantages of speed, surprise, detection and flexibility to the commanders conducting war at sea. Naval aviation vastly increased the area of the sea on which a maritime power could exercise control and domination. While securing control of the sea and air, nations could deprive their adversary of the use of the sea and the sea lanes for trade, commerce and movement of troops.

The events of December 1971 brought about a tectonic shift in their mindsets, as Indians discovered for the first time the power of sea control and sea superiority in influencing and determining the geopolitical events of the region. India also saw the capability of the naval aviation when INS *Vikrant* and her jet fighter and anti-submarine squadrons, operating miles from the shore of the adversary, imposed India's national will and obtained favourable results. Admiral S.M. Nanda wrote about the 1971 Indo-Pak War: 'Our unqualified success in conducting carrier operations in 1971, and the *Vikrant*'s outstanding contribution to winning the war so quickly and decisively, acted as a tremendous morale booster for our fledgling Navy, which counts itself among the less than ten marine nations that have the operational expertise and wherewithal to maintain and operate aircraft carriers.[4]

This knowledge now forms an important part of the strategy and policy for the long-term defence planning of India. The assets that can bring about effective sea control take decades of planning to acquire or build. The aircraft carriers, naval aircraft, submarines and craft are complex capital equipment that have a long lead time of designing, building, proving and supply. More significantly, it also takes time to develop trained and skilled manpower and institutional capabilities to operate such assets and maintain them; they need large capital investment too, and past experience shows that the lead time from projecting the need for such capital assets to its acceptance, identification of the assets, their materialization and deployment in active service may be of the order of 20 to 25 years, sometimes even longer. For example, India was evaluating the British jet trainer Hawk in the early 1980s, but its acquisition took place almost 30 years later. A nation aspiring to be in league with the world powers to exercise sea control and project power beyond its shores must take steps to build a strong navy. The story of arriving at this realization through the war of 1971 has been covered in this book.

This book has been divided into three parts. The first is a brief comparative history of navigation in India and with the Western powers. It also discusses the development of the Indian Navy post-Independence and the acquisition of INS *Vikrant*, one of the ships that played a key role in the 1971 war.

The second part narrates the events of the 1971 war from our perspective, from on board INS *Vikrant*. It covers the preparations for war, the conflicts on the western front in the Arabian Sea, and life on board the *Vikrant* on the eastern front.

[4]Nanda, S.M., *The Man Who Bombed Karachi: A Memoir*, HarperCollins Publishers India, 2004, p. 285.

The third and final part covers the aftermath of the war and the fallout for both India and Pakistan. It also discusses the legacy of the Indian Navy's contributions to this war.

The White Tigers squadron INAS 300 celebrates its birth anniversary on 7 July each year in commemoration of its commissioning on 7 July 1960 in the UK. July 2000 marked the fortieth anniversary, and the squadron had decided to celebrate it in Goa. All erstwhile White Tigers were invited. I had retired from the Indian Navy by then, but I too received an invite and thus went to Goa. There I saw many old veterans who were on board INS *Vikrant* in December 1971 and had taken part in the 1971 war. Rear Admiral S.K. Gupta was one of them.

We were accommodated in a seaside hotel close to the naval airbase. I had by then been thinking about writing about the Indo-Pak War of 1971. I was much impressed by the spectacular outcome of the 1971 war and strongly felt that India should analyse the conduct of the war and establish what India and the Indian armed forces did right to win the war so decisively. I felt that the role played by the Indian Navy in the war had added a special dimension to it. The Indian Navy's domination of the Arabian Sea and the Bay of Bengal had caused the quick capitulation of our adversary. I discussed my thoughts with Rear Admiral Gupta over a dinner, but I felt I was not able to infect him with my enthusiasm.

On my return, I began to work on the theme and started to research and write. I contacted many retired officers and sailors, and talked to them about their experiences of the 1971 war. I began to read about the *Vikrant*, Sea Hawks and Alizés. I read other works published on the subject. In 2018, I felt I was ready. I contacted Rear Admiral Gupta once again. He was now living in Bengaluru. Surprisingly, he remembered our discussions from 2000 in Goa. He listened to me on the phone patiently, but I could sense he was still not enthused. He said he did not have his flying log books and notes from 1971. We have had a good personal bonding from our days in the squadron. It took me about a year to get him to agree to co-author the book with me, and what you now hold in your hands is the result.

PART ONE

1

Power over the Sea:
A Brief History

As an ancient nation, India, the land of the Indus River, has been dealing with invaders and enemies since time immemorial. Right from the times of ancient kingdoms, security from outsiders has been the priority for rulers, as witnessed by works such as the *Arthashastra*. Yet, despite its expansive coastline and the many rivers that run through the subcontinent, Indian defence systems remained woefully lopsided.

Traditionally, India understood the use of land and land routes used by the invaders over centuries for both invasions and occupations; they were also able to put up some measure of defence against such invasions. But India did not grasp the nature of seas and the oceans, and their influence and interplay with the security of the land. Apart from some exploration towards Southeast Asia by the Chola kings in the South, most naval explorations in India were limited to coastal excursions—for fishing and trade. Little effort was made in developing a marine philosophy and strategy for the Indian seas. Inculcating a marine tradition and raising an effective marine force capable of operating at a distance from the Indian shores to establish control of seas around India was never a priority. The sea was traditionally viewed as benign and a guarantor of the security of the subcontinent. Indians seemed to be convinced that no harm could come to India from the direction of the seas. We do not see in the past centuries any excursions or explorations to match or come even close to those of the European seafaring nations, such as Portugal, Spain, France and England.

Western powers expanded their maritime capabilities from the fifteenth century onwards. The knowledge and experience gained from the sailing expeditions and voyages of Vasco da Gama, Christopher Columbus, John Hawkins, Francis Drake, Walter Raleigh and others like them, eventually determined the world order. Tapping into this newfound power, the seafaring nations occupied Asia, Africa, the two Americas, and large and small islands in the oceans. They ruled, colonized and influenced international trade. Despite all this, India and the Indians failed to see the sea for what it was, and for this fault, Indians paid with occupation and slavery under the European nations.

Arthur Herman, a popular American historian, wrote in his book *To Rule the Waves*:

> An American Captain, Alfred Mahan, was the first to assert that the history of Western civilization has been the history of sea power; the ability of states and empires to exert control over the 'wide common' of the oceans, and deny it to others. Through sea power even a small nation could dominate its neighbours, by controlling their access to resources while securing its own, and even a small nation could bend events, trends, geography, the globe itself to its will. This is the essence of what it means to 'Rule the Waves'.[1]

---

[1] Herman, Arthur, *To Rule the Waves: How the British Navy Shaped the Modern World*, New York, HarperCollins, 2004, p. xvii.

How Britain Became the Master of the Seas

Despite being a fairly small nation, Britain was able to expand its naval powers. Perhaps, being an island heightened its awareness of the power of the sea. The growth in the British Navy was such that it overtook all the navies of the European mainland in almost no time and became the supreme ruler of the seas.

Britain ruled the waves with unchallenged superiority. In 1694, Lord Halifax of Britain said, 'The first article of an Englishman's political creed must be, that he believeth in the sea.'[2] This sums up the national creed of Britain and its pursuit of maritime power expressed in the words 'Britannia, rules the waves'. How this came about is an interesting story in itself.

Colonial expansion has its origins in the global spice trade, which involved buying spices from the East and selling to the thriving markets in Europe. The scarcity of Indian spices in Europe presented lucrative opportunities for European spice merchants, but the supply route of spices from India was blocked by Turkey, leaving no alternative land route to India. To overcome this problem, Portugal decided to send a fleet of ships led by the experienced master mariner Vasco da Gama, who landed on the western coast of India at Calicut on 20 May 1498. He had successfully established a sea route from Europe to India by sailing south from Europe in the Atlantic Ocean and then going around the Cape of Good Hope to enter the Indian Ocean.

Vasco da Gama and his men began to purchase the spices they had come in search of. There was, however, a dispute between the visitors from Europe and the local Indian merchants when Vasco da Gama and his compatriots did not want to pay the customs duty on the goods purchased. They also refused to pay for goods in gold as was the custom of trading between foreigners

---

[2]Clipson, Jim, 'The Naval History Blog: No. 3', *Port Towns & Urban Cultures*, 30 January 2017, https://tinyurl.com/r8py7vkb. Accessed on 2 August 2023.

and Indian merchants. Instead, they wanted to pay for the spices by barter of some goods they had brought with them. This was not acceptable to the Indian traders, who wanted payment in gold or silver.

Bitter quarrels ensued. Vasco da Gama retreated but returned with a larger and more powerful fleet of warships. The Portuguese ships bombarded the Indian establishments. They overpowered the local rulers and established themselves on pockets of Indian land along the western coast. This was the beginning of a Western power dominating the Indian seas.

Portugal ruled the waves in the Atlantic Ocean, Indian Ocean, Arabian Sea, Bay of Bengal, Strait of Malacca and Sri Lanka for about a hundred years. Later, Portugal formed a union with Spain in Europe. Then on, Spain declared itself the master of the Indian seas. Meanwhile, the rivalry between Spain and Britain peaked in Europe, where Spain was the superior maritime and naval power of the time, while the British ships remained a thorn in their side with constant raids and looting of their goods.

In 1598, Spain planned a naval invasion of Britain from the southern coast in the English Channel to defeat them once and for all. The British fleet was much smaller than the Spanish Armada, which comprised 130 ships. However, their smaller ships were more agile and were led by brilliant sailors, like Sir Francis Drake and John Hawkins. The English inflicted a crushing defeat on the invincible Spanish Armada and destroyed most of their ships.

With its major European rival in Europe defeated and neutralized, the British became the dominant colonial power. The British East India Company was founded in 1600 by enterprising Englishmen. Most importantly, they obtained exclusive rights to trade in India and the East Indies. The royal charter granted to the company included the right to wage war.

However, this trade was so lucrative that tensions continued between European nations for the right to trade in India and the East Indies. It spilled over into their naval units and trading centres established on the Indian shores. After the Spanish, their principal contender in India was the French. Full-scale hostilities among these European nations carried on till 1805, when the British fleet led by Admiral Horatio Nelson gave a crushing defeat to the French naval fleet of Napoleon Bonaparte, in the Battle of Trafalgar. This was followed by sea battles between the French and the British on the eastern coast of India in which the French naval fleet led by Governor General Joseph François Dupleix was defeated.

This began the unhindered British rule of the Indian Ocean and the Indian subcontinent for nearly 150 years till the Second World War, when the baton of the dominant *numero uno* world sea power passed from the British to the US. This situation continues to the present.

Feet on the Ground

Even while Britain ruled the waves of the oceans and seas surrounding India, they conducted themselves as landsmen. They ruled India with a large army, and an equally big police force, both raised by recruiting the men from amongst the Indians themselves. This was no different from the Mughals, who, too, had ruled India for 200 years with land armies raised from the Indian population. The sea around India was not considered a threat. Instead, the sea was regarded as a protective frontier on three sides of the Indian subcontinent, which along with the great Himalayas in the north provided protection to India from foreign invaders. In all the British campaigns, big and small, from the Battle of Plassey in 1757 to the defeat of Mysore, Hyderabad, Marathas, Sikhs, Awadh, and the 1857 War of Independence, the Indians confronted only the British armies. The perception of British as a land-based power took hold and continued till India gained independence in August 1947. This impression did not break even during the two world wars. The true nature and identity of the British as the world sea power remained concealed from the Indian mind.

Since the sea was considered sufficient protection against invasion, this left only the land in the northwest as a threat. It was indeed this direction from which the invaders had started invading India, in as far back as 326 BCE, when Alexander attacked India from the same northwestern route. Starting from Greece, Alexander had moved in the easterly direction, subduing regions on the way, then crossing the mighty Indus River with his army to reach Punjab, where he faced King Puru. It was a battle that left him unable to launch another conquest. Subsequent invasions of India over the next 2,000 years came from Iran and Afghanistan following the same route. Invaders like Muhammad Ghori, Nadir Shah, Ahmad Shah Abdali and others followed, and so did Babur.

Though the British broke the pattern and made their forays into India by sea, their effective land domination made this aspect of their prowess a distant memory for Indians. This was because the British began as traders but became politically ambitious when they noticed that the central authority of the Mughal Empire in India had become weak and untenable. With the weakening of the Mughal emperors after the death of Aurangzeb in 1707, the governors of the provinces far from Delhi, which was the capital, had become autocratic and declared themselves autonomous. The governor of Bengal was one such example. The new British East India Company raised a small army of local soldiers, and fought and defeated the Nawab in 1757 in the Battle of Plassey (in Bengal). This was the beginning of the British rule of Bengal, first by proxy and later directly. They continued and occupied regions along the coastline of India initially before moving inland. In the next 100 years, they colonized the entire country.

The British took care to build large forts in Calcutta (now Kolkata), Madras and Bombay on the sea coast of India to protect their trading establishments and settlements. All their ships came to India and left from behind these forts. Even here, the common people did not see what the British ships brought to India and what they carried away. The high walls and ramparts of the British forts concealed from the public view the activities of arrival, departure, loading and unloading of the British ships on the waterfronts. This added to the perception that Britain was a land power.

Most Indians who lived far from the sea shores never saw the maritime prowess of the British ships and their legendary might at sea. It was always the British army and their soldiers who came in contact with them. The British seemed like a race who had their feet firmly on the ground. The situation did not change much after Independence either. A recent study of the Royal Indian Navy suggests, 'The post-independent Indian Government's defence policy was mainly focused on the land frontier and most of the naval proposals were turned down, as the Government failed to understand the importance of a balanced naval force in the Indian Ocean.'[3]

Colonial Times

Like the navies of other European nations before them, the British Royal Navy was the lifeline of the British colonizers operating from India, as Britain was situated thousands of miles away from the Indian mainland, and there was no established land route from India to England. In the eighteenth and the nineteenth centuries, the one-way passage around the Cape of Good Hope took months of sailing at high seas to reach Europe, covering a distance of 10,720 miles (from Bombay). This journey was safe and secure because the British Royal Navy was the

---

[3]Mohanan, Kalesh, *The Royal Indian Navy; Trajectories, Transformations and the Transfer of Power,* Routledge, 2021.

unquestioned power in the Atlantic and the Indian oceans. Most of the crucial sea control points in the Atlantic Ocean, Indian Ocean, Red Sea, Strait of Malacca and the Mediterranean Sea were held and controlled by the British Royal Navy. Gibraltar, Port Said, Malacca, Singapore, Suez Canal, Aden, Trincomalee, Colombo, Karachi, Bombay, Madras, Calcutta and Mauritius were all in British territory, from where Britain could monitor and control the passage of ships and trade traffic, both friendly and unfriendly. The British grip over the Indian subcontinent had become stronger with the construction of the Suez Canal in 1869, which connected the Mediterranean Sea and the Red Sea. It shortened the voyage from London to Bombay, bringing it down to 6,260 miles.

The British knew and understood how vital and important a strong navy was to them and the unique advantage it gave them. They guarded their fleet and their naval expertise, and took care not to share their maritime skills with Indians for fear of raising competition. They avoided hiring the natives from their colonies for responsible positions on the Royal Navy ships. If unavoidable, they only hired the Indians for low-level manual jobs on their ships. They regarded maritime skills as special expertise that had enabled them to gain territorial control of the Indian subcontinent.

However, they could not do without local manpower. The ships of the seventeenth century used wind and stretched canvas to propel themselves in the water during their voyages over the seas. When compared to the ships of today, these were relatively small and could carry only a small number of people. The British needed manpower to manage and control the large territory and equally large number of Indian people. They also needed agents to collect revenue and taxes. It was a huge logistical problem. They could not transport the needed numbers of suitably trained and qualified men from Britain to India due to the distance and the size of ships.

To overcome this problem, among other things, they introduced their own education system in India, so that the local people could begin to read and write in English. The British needed them in India as their office clerks, junior accountants and other such jobs. To conduct warfare in India, they recruited Indians as soldiers and called them the native British army, which worked under the command of British officers and superintendents. This system worked in the early years, but turned out to be a double-edged sword, as this large body of Indian population, educated and trained by the British, eventually became an instrument for the campaigns among the Indian population to force the British to leave India.

The British had divided the naval defence of India into two categories. First was for the defence of mainland India against attack or invasion by an enemy of the British Empire from the sea. To counter this threat, the British Royal Navy was given the responsibility of protecting the Indian subcontinent. The eastern fleet of the Royal Navy was based in Sri Lanka at the port of Trincomalee to guard the approaches to India from the Indian Ocean or from the east through the Strait of Malacca. The second category was the local defence of the Indian coastline and merchant shipping. This was a small task and required only a modest naval force. The British initially called this force the Royal Indian Marine (RIM), but later renamed it as Royal Indian Navy or the RIN. The RIN had no responsibility of defending India from external threat or aggression, as this was squarely the responsibility of the British Royal Navy controlled from London. Instead, the RIN functioned along the coastline alone.

The Birth of an Indian Naval Force

The British raised three large armies of Indians with which they subjugated and ruled India. These were armies of Bengal,

Bombay and Madras. Later, they merged them to form one single British Indian Army. Surprisingly, they did not display similar enthusiasm to raise a native navy from the local population and kept the maritime functions exclusive to themselves. Changing geopolitics in Europe increased the threat at home from other European nations, so Britain needed the Royal Navy in Britain for reasons of security, protection and deterrence. Unlike other European nations, the British did not possess a large standing army at home.

Even though the Royal Navy had to leave Indian shores, the British just chose not to raise a proper full-time Indian navy. Perhaps, they perceived in it a potential threat to the Royal Navy and, therefore, a threat to the British colonization of India. The importance the British attached to the Indian navy at that time is illustrated by the fact that the budget for the RIM was controlled by the British Indian Army. The defence budget provided for the army and the air force, leaving little or nothing for the navy. This was the humble beginning of a naval force that, 40 years later, took the shape of the RIN, with the passing of the Indian Navy (Discipline) Act in 1934.

The British were particularly careful to keep the RIN away from the role of defence of the seas around India and the sea lines of communication (SLOC)[4] in the Arabian Sea and the Indian Ocean. The naval defence of India was kept as the responsibility of the British Royal Navy headquartered in Britain. For this, the British government of India paid a fixed sum of £100,000 annually to Britain from the Indian exchequer. This payment continued till 1913, when, with the prospect of a world war breaking out staring them in the face, the British decided to increase the strength of ships to be deployed for the naval defence of India. To

---

[4]SLOC is a term describing the primary maritime routes between ports, used for trade, logistics and naval forces. It is generally used in reference to naval operations to ensure that SLOCs are open, or closed in times of war.

meet this cost, India had to pay £1,680,000 to Britain as capital outlay to acquire more warships, and £490,000 as annual payment against £100,000 earlier. Britain laid down a stipulation that this enhanced provision in the Indian budget would be utilized to build ships for India, but these warships, though funded with Indian money, would operate under the control of the Royal Navy and, if needed, they would be requisitioned by the latter for operational deployment. This was the situation that lasted through the First World War till the Second World War, which brought about significant changes in the world order.

2

India Inherits a Navy

Following the Quit India Movement of 1942, the British government had made a commitment to the Indian leaders spearheading the freedom struggle that they would grant a dominion status to India after the Second World War. However, once the War ended with victory of the Allies, this promise did not materialize. An event occurred in the closing years of the Second World War, and another one year after the War ended in 1945, which set the alarm bells ringing for the British government in India.

The first event was the spirited armed fight put up by the Azad Hind Fauj, also known as the Indian National Army or INA, led by Subhas Chandra Bose. During the Second World War, Japanese army captured the British colony at Singapore in February 1942, taking the British army officers and men as prisoners, with many of them being Indians. Next, Japanese army continued to advance eastward and invaded Burma, another British colony, and occupied Burma too. They then moved to India's northeastern borders from Burma side to attack British India. At this time, the Indians were waging a freedom struggle against the British.

Subhas Chandra Bose was at the forefront of this freedom movement. He was of the view that the British would not depart from India unless they were ousted by force. He thus left India to garner support from the international community. When Singapore fell to the Japanese army, Bose approached the Japanese to permit the Indian POWs to join him and form the INA and attack the British in India alongside the Japanese army. The Japanese agreed, and the Indian officers and soldiers held by the Japanese were released to join Bose's INA. However, the British Indian army was able to halt the advances of the Japanese army and forced them to retreat from the northeastern borders, back to Burma.

The British Indian army followed the retreating Japanese and retook Burma from the Japanese. The Japanese army was eventually defeated when the allied forces dropped atom bombs on the Japanese cities of Hiroshima and Nagasaki in 1945. Along with the Japanese army, Bose's INA was also defeated. Bose died in an air crash and the senior members of the INA were captured and brought to India by the British. They were tried for treason at the Red Fort from November 1945–May 1946. Their trial gave rise to patriotic fervour in India. A strong wave of resentment against the British, bordering on hatred, swept India and the British dreaded for their safety. They feared there might be a violent uprising against them, just like in 1857.

The second triggering event was the RIN uprising in February 1946 in Bombay, in which the Indians serving in the RIN mutinied against the British officers. They had been getting served bad quality of food and were also suffering because of abusive racial behaviour of the British. The situation took an alarming turn when few protesters took over some of the RIN ships, inspired by the heroism of the INA. In less than 48 hours, 20,000 men took over 78 ships and craft, and 21 shore establishments. They replaced British flags with Indian ones. The British retaliated. The rebelling sailors trained the guns of the captured ships towards the Gateway of India, threatening to blow it away. The British panicked. Such was the fury and scale of this resistance that the uprising began to spread to the units of the British Indian Air

Force and the British Indian Army. These two events and their widespread anti-British fallout made the British see the writing on the wall—the Empire wouldn't last for long in India.

The memorial plaque in Bombay erected for the RIN uprising aptly acknowledges this truth: 'Their contribution in February 1946 proved to be a turning point that hastened India's Independence.'[1] The then British Prime Minister (PM) Clement Attlee had said, while answering a question, that the INA and the RIN mutiny of 1946 had forced the British to leave India, while the impact of the 1942 Quit India Movement had been 'minimal'.[2]

Regardless of the motivating cause, India was finally gaining freedom and was set to become an independent nation. Key to this process was one man: Lord Louis Mountbatten.

Mountbatten Arrives

When the British government decided to end its rule in India and hand over power to the Indians, British PM Attlee proposed a bill in the British Parliament. On 18 February 1947, the British House of Commons in London voted by an overwhelming majority 'to end British rule in India no later than June 1948'[3]. To do the job, Attlee chose and appointed 46-year-old Louis Mountbatten as the last Viceroy of India in place of the incumbent Viceroy Archibald Wavell.

Louis Mountbatten was of the British royal lineage. He was the fourth child of Britain's sovereign Queen Victoria's granddaughter.

---

[1]Mohanan, Kalesh, *The Royal Indian Navy: Trajectories, Transformations and the Transfer of Power*, Routledge, 2019, p. 169.

[2]Sadasyula, Ratnakar, 'The Forgotten Naval Mutiny of 1946 and India's Independence', *Swarajya*, 26 January 2022, https://tinyurl.com/3364s5ff. Accessed on 1 August 2023.

[3]Lapierre, Dominique, and Larry Collins, *Freedom at Midnight*, Vikas Publishing House, 1976, p. 53.

In his youth, Mountbatten had chosen the career of a naval officer. In 1943, during the Second World War, Winston Churchill, the then British PM, was looking for a 'young and vigorous mind'[4] when he chose Mountbatten and appointed him as the supreme allied commander of Southeast Asia. Mountbatten was leading the Allied campaign in Burma in 1945 when the War ended. Thereafter, he rose to become the first sea lord of the Royal Navy in 1955, admiral of the fleet in 1956, and chief of the defence staff (UK) and chairman of the Chiefs of Staff Committee in 1959. Mountbatten enjoyed a brilliant naval career, which was significant to his stint in India later.

Prime Minister Attlee assigned Mountbatten to handle the transfer of power in India. Mountbatten left England by air on 20 March 1947 to take up his new appointment and arrived in India two days later. He was sworn as the twentieth and last Viceroy of India on 24 March 1947, in a ceremony held in the Durbar Hall of the Viceroy's House in New Delhi, now known as the Rashtrapati Bhavan, the official residence of the President of India. Mountbatten had the mandate to transfer power to India by June 1948. On arriving in India, he had 16 months to complete his mission.

The situation in India was volatile and passions were running high. The outgoing 64-year-old Wavell briefed the new Viceroy on the gravity of the situation in India. Wavell did not rule out communal riots. He added that he was worried about the British in India because the loyalty of the armed forces and the police had come under suspicion. They could not be trusted or relied upon to safeguard the British men, women and children. In the politically, racially and communally charged atmosphere in India, there was widespread and strong antipathy for the British. The atmosphere was particularly volatile due to the arousal of communal passions between the Hindu and the Muslim communities over

---

[4]Ibid.

the partition of the country, following the two-nation theory of Muhammad Ali Jinnah, the Muslim League leader. The painful memories of the 1857 mutiny still haunted the British. The sum total of Wavell's advice to Mountbatten was that India was akin to a tinder box, and a small accidental spark could start a fire. It was difficult to tell what form the conflagration would take. Wavell informed Mountbatten of the emergency measures that he had planned to put in operation at the highest levels if it became necessary to evacuate the British nationals and their families in India to a safe destination outside the country. These measures were now for Mountbatten to consider.

He studied and evaluated the political situation in India. He, too, was alarmed at the bitterness and acrimony among the political rivals in the Indian political landscape. There were reports of an increasing frequency of violence and breakdown of law and order in different parts of India. British intelligence was also reporting of the disaffection in the armed forces against the British. The naval mutiny of February 1946 by the sailors of the RIN had shaken the British to the core. In this surcharged atmosphere in the country, Mountbatten felt that June 1948 was too far away. He, therefore, decided to advance the date of transfer of power by 10 months, choosing 15 August 1947. It is said that Mountbatten chose this date because the Second World War had ended with the announcement of the surrender of Japan to the Allies on 15 August 1945. On that day, Mountbatten was in Burma, leading the Allied campaign to drive out the Japanese forces from Burma. Hence, the date was significant for him.

India became independent on 15 August 1947, but the outgoing British were able to persuade the Indian leadership for India to remain in the British Commonwealth. As per this arrangement, Viceroy Mountbatten was reappointed as the first Governor General of India from 15 August 1947. He had the mandate from the British government to stay in India till June 1948. As the constitutional head of the government, he utilized the remaining 10 months of his stay in India to aid and assist the new Indian government in taking important decisions. He left India in June 1948 and C. Rajagopalachari succeeded him as the next governor general of India on 21 June 1948. This was a period of great significance, as the shape of the young democracy and its various institutions was being determined. Among them were the armed forces: the Indian Army, IAF and the Indian Navy.

Military Implications of Partition

One of the decisions Mountbatten took was to implement the plan of partition of India, segregating the Muslim majority regions into a different nation, Pakistan. In April 1947, the British Indian government had accepted that the partition of the country would also involve the division of the armed forces. Following this decision, the ships and craft held by the RIN were divided between India and Pakistan. India received two-thirds of the assets, with Pakistan getting one-third.[5] The naval assets that India received included two frigates, four sloops, one corvette and some minesweepers, tugs, harbour defence motor launches and miscellaneous craft. The two big ships of this lot were of just 1,300 tons displacement each. They did not count much in terms of offensive or defensive capabilities. Indian Navy's effective manpower strength in July 1948 was 5,242, which included 408 officers.[6]

Prior to 15 August 1947, most of the infrastructure of the RIN was shared between Bombay and Karachi. With the division of India, the port city of Karachi, situated at the northeastern

---

[5]The process and the manner of division have been described in interesting detail in the book: Collins, Larry, and Dominique Lapierre, *Freedom at Midnight*, HarperCollins, 1975.

[6]Mohanan, Kalesh, *The Royal Indian Navy: Trajectories, Transformations and the Transfer of Power*, Routledge, 2019, p. 202.

corner of the Arabian Sea, along with all the naval (basic and professional) training establishments functioning from there, went to Pakistan. The division of assets with Pakistan affected some departments of Indian Navy more adversely. For example, 70 per cent of the senior communication branch sailors in the undivided navy were Muslims and they opted to go to Pakistan, and that led to a serious shortage in the branch. Marine engineering was another crucial branch that was hit hard. Its strength of 108 officers before Partition reduced to 35 after the division. To add to the problems, most training establishments to train officers and men of the navy were situated in Karachi, now in Pakistan, and the equivalents were yet to start functioning in India.

From Partition onwards, the two navies took different directions. There were multiple factors that determined the direction that the Indian Navy took. The more important of these were the extremely dilapidated state of the Indian economy; poor state of the Indian Navy; the meagre assets inherited from the British rulers; availability of the eight partially completed light aircraft carriers lying mothballed in the UK since the end of the war in 1945; non-availability of suitably qualified senior Indian Naval officers to take over the reins of Indian Navy and the vast security needs of a country the size of India. All these problems were eventually resolved, as we shall see.

Since the British utilized the services of Indians for low-level work but refrained from employing them at higher posts in military and civil services, in August 1947, commander was the highest rank held by an Indian naval officer: Cdr Ram Dass Katari. All the senior officers in the RIN above the rank of commander were British. As a result of the transfer of power in August 1947, most of the British officers of the RIN opted to leave India and go back to their home country, Britain.

The RIN advised against accelerated and speedy indigenization by quicker promotion to Indian naval officers because they did not have the age, rank, years of naval service and experience needed for the higher ranks. The advice was not wrong. It simply stated a fact. From the service norms available, it was well known that it took about 35 years of naval service for an officer in the Royal Navy to reach the rank of rear admiral. This was another problem that would have to be addressed and adequately resolved. Before that, the British involvement in the development of the navy and their motivation behind the same need to be understood.

The Democracy's Armed Forces: A British Force in India?

The Allies won the Second World War, but the six-year War had considerably drained and weakened Britain all round, especially its economy. According to some estimates, by the end of the Second World War, Britain had amassed an immense debt of £21 billion. In the pre-War years, Britain was the acknowledged superior sea power of the world, enjoying the encomiums and titles such as 'Britannia, rules the waves'. Their power was such that they were able to maintain global peace to an extent, leading to the creation of the term 'Pax Britannica'. By the time the six-year World War ended, Britain had ceded its number one position to the US—Pax Americana had replaced Pax Britannica. Britain had a large number of capital warships, like aircraft carriers, cruisers, battle ships and destroyers, which were rendered surplus to its security needs after the War. Suddenly, there was no enemy to fight against in faraway oceans and distant lands.

When withdrawing from India, the British nurtured an ambition to retain control of the Indian armed forces even after India became free. They wanted to continue to use India as their power base in the Far East; to achieve this end, they wanted to retain control of the Indian armed forces in the form of a united defence force based in India, but under the command and control of Britain, so as to maintain their influence in the Indian Ocean.

They wanted India to formally outsource its defence needs to Britain. They, therefore, made all efforts to persuade India to join the British Commonwealth, which was the route for such a proposal to fructify. They had planned to negotiate a military treaty with India as per which India would transfer some land parcels on the Indian coastline to the British to maintain this united defence force.

The British were convinced that India did not need to raise and maintain an independent navy comparable to the British Royal Navy. The image (of 'Britannia, rules the waves') from the previous century of Pax Britannica still lingered. The British were of the view that India should maintain a small coastal navy, and for its larger national security needs, it should attach itself to the apron strings of a major naval power, by which, of course, they meant Britain. A study conducted at the request of the Government of India in 1948 concluded in its report that it did not envisage a large navy for India.[7] It recommended that the Indian Navy should be planned as complementary to some great power. According to this report, it would have been most efficient for India to look after the coast and local defence, and leave the defence of the seas to Britain and the Royal Navy. The proposal did not cut ice with the Indian leadership and the British plan did not see the light of day.

A Lack of Vision and Expertise

While the British were pursuing their agenda, the leadership of the new independent India felt the need for a strong army and air force.

The first budget of India after Independence covered about 7.5 months, from 15 August 1947 to 31 March 1948. It was a

---

[7]Mohanan, Kalesh, *The Royal Indian Navy: Trajectories, Transformations and the Transfer of Power*, Routledge, 2021, p. 219.

budget deficit, showing revenue of ₹171 crore and expenditure of ₹197 crore. It highlighted the dire straits of the Indian economy and of the country's defence and security apparatus, which the British had handed over when they left. The budget allocated ₹92.74 crore, or 47 per cent of the expenditure to defence.[8] This amount was allocated entirely to the army and air force.

However, there was no matching ambition or desire for raising an Indian Navy despite the fact that the Royal Navy, which had protected India from an attack from the sea till 1947, was set to retreat from the Indian shores, lock, stock and barrel.

India is a subcontinent with a more than 7,500 km-long coastline of the mainland and a 2,100-km coastline of her island territories. In addition, India has 43,230 sq. km of coastal wetlands to secure and defend. There are also the SLOCs to be taken care of. In the pre-Independence years, the British government had assigned the role of local defence of the Indian coastline to the RIN, and its responsibilities included marine surveys, maintenance of lighthouses and transportation of troops. The primary responsibility of defence of India against any major aggression and invasion from sea was assigned to the Royal Navy. After Independence, free India had to assume responsibility for both these functions. The low priority given to the Indian Navy by the British government can be gauged from a report of a committee set up to augment and enhance the Indian armed forces. A sum of ₹45.09 crore was recommended by the committee for the development of the defence forces of colonial India and the share of the RIN recommended was a mere ₹2.62 crore, or 5.8 per cent of the total outlay.[9]

The role of the Indian Navy of independent India continued to be to protect merchant shipping and the Indian coastline.

---

[8]Union Budget 1947–48, presented by Finance Minister R.K. Shanmukham Chetty
[9]Mohanan, Kalesh, *The Royal Indian Navy: Trajectories, Transformations and the Transfer of Power*, Routledge, 2019, p. 41.

The RIN functioned more like a coastal navy, having little or no role on the high seas. The main task of defending the Indian subcontinent, which was with the Royal Navy till 15 August 1947, should have been assumed by the Indian Navy of independent India. But the Indian Navy continued to be entrusted with the task of protecting shipping and the seacoast of India during the 1962 and 1965 wars as was the practice during the pre-1947 years.

It is evident from the list of ships and craft allocated to India and Pakistan that in the pre-1947 years, the RIN did not have any element of aviation, although the Fleet Air Arm (FAA) formed an important operational branch of the Royal Navy of the UK since the Second World War. Incidentally, it also did not have a submarine or a submarine arm. India got its first submarine INS *Kalvari* in December 1967, 20 years after Independence.

However, the need for a navy for the security and defence of India had not figured in anyone's calculations, neither among the Indian political philosophers and naval thinkers nor the political leadership. This was the situation despite the proof that Indian waters needed protection. Andaman and Nicobar Islands, situated in the Bay of Bengal, away from the mainland, had been effortlessly invaded and occupied by the Japanese naval forces in 1942 during the Second World War. The Japanese held these islands for three years till 1945. After Independence, the vast archipelago of Andaman and Nicobar Islands belonged to India and they needed to be secured.

In the century leading up to Independence, Indians had been preoccupied with the freedom struggle against the British. Indians did not have any expertise of ruling and governing their vast land and its 39 crore people (which was India's population in 1947). Worst of all, they neither had the knowledge nor the experience of how to protect their land and people from external threats and invasions.

There is, therefore, little surprise that the Indian government also lacked the vision, thought and experience in raising, operating and maintaining a viable standing naval force of seagoing warships. Apart from the massive capital investment needed to make or buy warships, India did not have any idea about the complexity of raising and training the skilled manpower to operate and maintain a regular navy. Unlike the European countries, there was neither a realization of the necessity nor a dream or aspiration for a marine tradition.

Also, India only had little idea about the dedicated infrastructure of ship construction yards; the special steel needed to build seagoing warships; specialized dockyards; maintenance and repair facilities; as well as setting up of the auxiliary industries linked to supporting the seagoing modern warships. The submarine arm and naval aviation are recognized branches of any modern navy, but these were totally unknown to the Indians. Indians were also barely aware of the vast investments needed to secure India; and even if they were to know this, where were the funds to come from? The country's coffers were empty, with the primary focus being on feeding the population. Moreover, who would undertake the urgent task of building independent India? Where was the especially skilled and experienced manpower? Where were the agencies that could undertake, understand and accomplish the nation-building task of such magnitude?

3

Building Up
an Indigenous Navy

When the Second World War ended, some 16 aircraft carriers were in the British shipyards in the UK, lying in a partially-built stage. Their construction was stopped mid-way in 1946 and their semi-built hulls were mothballed to stop incurring more expenditure. Vast sums of money were needed to operate and maintain the Royal Navy fleet as before and funds had become scarce. India, the jewel in the British crown, and a regular source of its boundless and bountiful riches and resources of all kinds for more than two centuries, was slipping away. Without India as its colony, it was doubtful if Britain, the small island nation of Europe, would remain viable. This was the question many in Britain were asking. The world order was changing fast and rearranging itself, and there was no place for a colonial power like Britain in it. Imperialism was dying and with it, the famous British Empire had come to an inglorious end. The sun was finally setting over the British Empire.

Funds for the Empire

To generate the much-needed funds to stabilize and resurrect its run-down and bleeding economy, Britain took many decisions. Among them, it decided to sell the second-hand, used capital warships of the Royal Navy to any country who would buy them. To ensure customers, Britain decided to sell them in ones and twos to the countries of the British Commonwealth. These countries were the former colonies of Britain, whom the latter had persuaded to remain with it and regard the British sovereign as their head. Britain, having fallen on bad times, was organizing a distress sale of family silver and national assets.

The British had first-hand knowledge of the state of the Indian Navy they had bequeathed to India. India had no navy worth the name, and it certainly was nowhere close to the size of the navy that independent India now needed, that too quite badly. India was, therefore, a promising candidate and a customer for the post-war sale of the second-hand warships of Britain's Royal Navy, provided Britain could persuade the new leadership of India to buy them. The fly in the ointment was the poor economy of free India. India would not be interested in the British bargains on offer, however attractive they seemed, because it just could not afford them. Whatever little money it had was needed to feed her people.

Nevertheless, the British doggedly persisted and pursued their suggestions and proposals through Lord Mountbatten till they were accepted and converted into sanctions and orders of the new Indian government. The decisions taken about the Indian Navy at the time, though at the instance of the British, proved beneficial for India in the next two decades.

As subsequent events followed, among other things, Mountbatten guided and steered the decisions of the Government of India for the purchase of two light aircraft carriers and associated aircraft from the UK for the Indian Navy of independent India.

These were the large ships built and acquired by the Royal Navy for use during the Second World War but had become redundant and expensive to maintain and operate in the post-War years.

A sale to India entailed two objectives: the British would dispose their surplus of the used large vessels, and they would commit India to future defence purchases and make it a client for the British industry of ships, submarines, aircraft carriers and aircraft. This would also create a long-term supplier-client relationship between the UK and India—a welcome prospect that could last half a century or more and resuscitate the ailing British economy.

The FAA had to be set up in the Indian Navy ab initio. The Indian Navy had neither the expertise nor the previous experience in this field. The training of the Indian Navy officers and men for naval aviation was a bigger and more daunting task than acquiring ships, aircraft and the associated wherewithal. With the transfer of power advanced by 10 months, the time available to Louis Mountbatten for the work he had planned for himself in India had shrunk.

Plan Paper No. 1

The RIN did not have an air element during the pre-Independence days. The events and the experiences of the Second World War proved the importance of the air element at sea. Triggered by this experience, in late 1947, the then Commander-in-Chief of the RIN, Vice Admiral Edward Parry, drew up a 10-year naval expansion plan. It also took into account the security needs of India at the sea for the next two to three decades. The Indian Navy was assigned a defensive role with the provision for acquiring an offensive capability.

This plan proposed immediate indigenization of the Indian Navy and its development to suit the needs and aspirations of independent India. It recommended the acquisition of two light aircraft carriers with complementary aircraft squadrons, an FAA, the needed shore establishments, three cruisers, eight destroyers, four submarines and other support ships that were necessary for training and auxiliary purposes. These projections were supported by Mountbatten and by PM Pandit Jawaharlal Nehru. The Government of India accepted and approved the recommendations made in the Plan Paper No. 1.

Shortage of trained, qualified and experienced officers and men needed for the expansion of the Indian Navy was a more serious problem than purchasing the hardware of ships and craft. After the transfer of power, the British officers and sailors were leaving India to go back home to Britain. Within weeks, the navy suddenly found itself bereft of key senior officers and sailors in critical billets. Indian officers and men of right experience and in adequate numbers were simply not available to man the rapid expansion of the Indian Navy and its new FAA. Mountbatten and other senior British officers, who were in top positions of the Indian Navy of free India, were moving fast with decisions, sanctions and approvals in the name of the Government of India.

It appeared from the pace of the events that the British were forcing the speed of decision-making. They were not only committing India to the purchase but also ensuring that people from India were selected and sent to the UK for training at various institutions and organizations. In November 1947, an Indian delegation visited the UK and made arrangements for 47 officers and 366 sailors of the Indian Navy to undergo various courses in Royal Navy establishments in the UK. The delegation also arranged for the Indian naval personnel to be attached to the ships of the Royal Navy fleet for hands-on practical sea training. For future planning of the Indian Navy, the delegation asked for the cost estimates of different types of new and second-hand ships, aircraft, support equipment, and their maintenance and operating costs. India needed cost and delivery information for the projections made in the Plan Paper No. 1.

This made it well-nigh impossible for the Indian government to backtrack on the purchase agreements and contracts five years or so down the line.

It is true that if the British had not forced the decision-making in 1947–48, it is doubtful whether the idea of setting up an Air Arm in the Indian Navy would have been conceptualized and pursued. India would have probably followed the development and expansion of the traditional surface navy. The events of 1971 proved the merits of the decision to set up an Air Arm of the Indian Navy. The British officers seconded to the Indian Navy from 1947–58 also worked hard to plan and equip the Indian naval aviation by organizing the training of naval pilots to fly in sea environment and from the Royal Navy aircraft carriers. The same applied to the training and skilling of the aircraft engineering personnel.

The Royal Navy officers also helped in creating the infrastructure of the planned naval air arm in India. This ensured that when INS *Vikrant*, the first aircraft carrier of India and her squadrons, arrived from the UK in 1961, the Indian Navy already had the rudiments of the infrastructure to receive and operate them. From the nucleus thus created, Indian naval aviation could build, develop and gain expertise in all departments of naval aviation—the most important being the flying operations of the fighter aircraft from the aircraft carrier, and training its own officers and men for flying and maintaining the naval aircraft. This skill set acquired over the next decade, from 1960–70, made Indian Navy unique in the South Asian region. India became the only country in the region to operate a carrier-based naval aviation in the 1960s.

To make up for the shortage of manpower, the Indian Navy expedited the recruitment of sailors. Between August 1948 and August 1949, 782 boys and 63 artificer apprentices were inducted. By August 1949, additional 1,632 direct entry sailors were recruited for other branches of the Indian Navy.

British Officers on Loan

Along with arranging for training of Indian officers in the UK, the Indian government joined hands with Britain to address the scarcity of trained and experienced manpower of naval officers and men of different seniority levels in different branches.

Persuaded by Lord Mountbatten, India agreed to make a request for loan of suitably qualified Royal Navy officers to manage the manpower crisis at hand. A Royal Navy officer was appointed as the first CNS of the Indian Navy. Under this arrangement, the Indian Navy had taken 69 Royal Navy officers on loan by the end of 1950. Three Royal Navy officers—Rear admiral Louis Mountbatten as the governor general, a Royal Navy admiral as the chief of the naval staff and another Royal Navy officer as the chief of naval aviation (CONA)—worked in tandem on the naval projects, especially the creation of the naval aviation. Rear Admiral J.T.S. Hall, a Royal Navy British officer, on loan to India, was selected by the Government of India to command and reorganize the RIN. He took up his appointment on 15 August 1947. He was re-designated as chief of the naval staff and commander-in-chief of the RIN. Hall assumed the new titles on 21 June 1948.

Cdr Ram Dass Katari was a cadet in 1931. In normal course, he would have qualified for the rank of rear admiral sometime in 1966. However, it was argued that since the Indian Navy is a smaller force compared to the Royal Navy, it would be possible to complete the process of indigenization in about 10 years, say by 1956. It was suggested that in the intervening period, senior British officers should be retained in the service or loaned from the Royal Navy. The British also let it be known that the transfer of British naval officers in the near future would reduce the number of trained and experienced officers to a dangerous level.

It was under these circumstances that India had to request the UK government to loan the services of senior Royal Navy officers for about 10 years from 1947. The arrangement was accepted and continued for 11 years from 1947 to 1958, when Vice Admiral Ram Dass Katari attained the right rank and seniority for appointment to the top post of the Indian Navy. He was the first Indian naval officer to be appointed as the CNS of the Indian Navy on 21 April 1958. Vice Admiral S.H. Carlill was the last British Royal Navy officer to serve as the CNS of the Indian Navy from 21 July 1955 to 21 April 1958.

Mountbatten's extensive experience in leading a mighty naval force came in useful in organizing the Indian Navy. Apart from the expertise he provided to the newly formed government, he was also able to guide the leadership on all military matters.

Under his guidance, India also agreed to acquire two aircraft carriers from Britain with carrier-borne squadrons of fighter aircraft to complement the carriers. The general traditional surface Indian Navy would purchase cruisers and destroyers to upgrade its strength. As a result, in the first year after Independence, cruisers and destroyers were acquired for the surface navy. INS *Jumna* and INS *Sutlej* were the Black Swan class of ships that had been commissioned in 1941. They were called the sloops of war. They displaced 1,300 tons each and were the biggest ships among the assets transferred to the Indian Navy.

In addition to the executive officers experienced in operating and handling large aircraft carriers, cruisers and destroyers, India needed qualified marine and electrical engineers to operate and maintain these large ships, the likes of which Indians had never operated before. India needed naval pilots to fly the fighter and anti-submarine aircraft from the aircraft carriers. There was a requirement to create a matching infrastructure on ground to support the new Indian Navy and the brand-new naval aviation. These projects that Mountbatten was asking India to embark on were ones of massive scope and complexity.

The upgradation of the Indian Navy was a mammoth task, unrivalled in reach, depth and complexity compared to any other the Indian Navy would undertake even later. It had become possible only because of the three professional Royal Navy officers handling the Indian Navy projects. The groundwork for the massive acquisition programme was laid, and its implementation began before Mountbatten left India upon completion of his tenure in June 1948. Well begun is half done. Within a span of 10 years, all the projects of the Indian Navy and the naval aviation that had been started in 1948–50 were completed or were approaching completion by 1960.

Mountbatten had achieved the massive task of planning the future Indian Navy in a short span of 10 months. From the expanse and the speed of decision-making in 1947–48, it is difficult not to reach the conclusion that this became possible only because Mountbatten was at the helm of affairs. He was a highly experienced senior naval officer of the Royal Navy by training and experience, which gave him the authority and professional acumen to draw the blueprint of the future Indian Navy and implement it in an incredibly short span of time. The sea was his first love and he planned the new Indian Navy with exemplary passion. He did not let the partisan interests of Britain colour his vision.

When it came to the Indian Navy, there were things he felt India would not be able to do for some time, as it lacked the expertise. Mountbatten took it upon himself to plan the path for them before he left office. That he was such a senior officer of the Royal Navy, who occupied the top post of viceroy and then the governor general of India, was a chance occurrence and a gift to the Indian Navy. Our navy's development at that time could not have been handled any better.

There is evidence[1] that when he was first approached in England and offered Viceroy's appointment in India, Mountbatten had not responded enthusiastically. He did not want to take up the job of transferring power from Britain to India. He resisted

---

[1] Lapierre, Dominique, and Larry Collins, *Freedom at Midnight*, Vikas Publishing House, 1976, p. 6.

and made demands just to be difficult, thinking he would be spared by PM Attlee and not be appointed to India. But PM Attlee had none of it. He was convinced that Mountbatten, and he alone, was the man for the difficult and disagreeable task of transferring power to India that lay ahead.

Had another person been appointed, such a person might have done the job of the transfer of power, but he would not have provided the knowledgeable guidance to plan, approve and implement the upgradation of the Indian Navy in just 10 months. India and the Indian Navy owe much to Mountbatten. It is almost certain that without Mountbatten, the new branch of naval aviation in the Indian Navy would have been stillborn.

Changes at Headquarters

In the pre-Independence period, as the role of the RIN was relatively minor, it was accordingly structured, equipped and organized. Rear Admiral Hall functioned as the flag officer, Bombay, and he oversaw the RIN. Apart from the few ships and craft, there were some training establishments, including a Directorate of Weapons and Training. Following Independence on 15 August 1947, some changes were made in recognition of the upheaval taking place in the RIN. This was when Rear Admiral Hall was promoted from the flag officer to command and head the RIN.

On 15 January 1949, the naval headquarters at New Delhi was reorganized into five main departments, each under a principal staff officer. These were: deputy CNS, chief of personnel, chief of administration, chief of material and CONA. The CONA was to look after the setting up of the FAA of the Indian Navy, also known as naval aviation.

Capt. H.C. Ranalds, a Royal Navy officer, was appointed the first CONA at the naval headquarters on 15 January 1949. He was followed by Capt. J.E. Smallwood RN on 16 November 1952 and Capt. C.E. Fenwick RN on 15 January 1955. Capt. R.H.P. Carver RN replaced Fenwick on 27 August 1956. Carver was replaced on 3 February 1959 by Commodore D.W. Kirke. He served as CONA for three-and-a-half years and was the last Royal Navy officer to serve as the CONA. Commodore George Douglas took over from Kirke as the first Indian naval officer to be appointed as the CONA. On 30 November 1966, CONA was re-designated as the assistant chief of naval staff (air).

Cdr Balbir Dutt Law, the first commanding officer of the squadron of Sea Hawk INAS 300, from 7 July 1960 to 12 January 1961, spoke about the development of the Air Arm of the Indian Navy with Rear Admiral S.K. Gupta:

> Naval headquarters continued to press for acquisition of an aircraft carrier and serious negotiations had begun with the admiralty. In 1956, a new CONA was appointed, Captain R.H.P. Carver, RN. The Air Arm owes much to this CONA during whose term all the detailed planning for acquiring and manning the aircraft carrier was undertaken. He was an officer with a distinguished war record and quickly moulded his team in New Delhi with determination and skill, to move forward. A new training programme was launched to prepare for the manning of the carrier and her operational squadrons. A small naval flying unit was established at Sulur, Coimbatore, to familiarize the aircrew and maintenance personnel with operating jet aircraft (de Havilland Vampires). Naval headquarters was also concerned about providing adequate shore facilities for the new carrier and her operational aircraft.
>
> At about this time, Captain Carver's period of secondment to the Indian Navy ended, and the admiralty deputed another RN officer who served at the naval headquarters until after the *Vikrant*'s arrival in India. The

appointment of CONA was upgraded from Captain to Commodore. The new CONA, Commodore D.W. Kirke, handled the work on *Vikrant* skilfully. The selection of all the different categories of personnel, their training at different establishments, the manufacture of ships, aircraft and equipment; the delivery, acceptance and positioning of aircraft at different air stations; workup of squadrons ashore; the trials and commissioning of the carrier; and finally, the workup of the ship and her squadrons, was a mammoth task to complete from a distance of 4,000 miles. This was all brilliantly executed by Commodore Kirke. At this stage, it was also clear that in the absence of an alternative site having been found, the existing facilities at Cochin (now Kochi) and Sulur would have to be improved to receive the frontline squadrons. Support facilities for the Alizés were established, and, more importantly, repair and overhaul facilities were extended to include the Sea Hawks.

Towards the end of 1959 and early 1960, our aircrew and maintenance personnel began to assemble at naval air stations in the UK and France, and commenced operational flying training on their newly-acquired aircraft. Most of the aircrew had no previous experience of operational flying. It was an enormous task to make each individual pilot fully proficient in the skills of using his aircraft as a weapon system, and also to mould the squadron and crews to fulfil the varying roles of naval air warfare. The frontline squadrons made excellent progress and achieved high standards in all aspects of air training and workup ashore.

The *Vikrant* Joins the Indian Navy

In India, the Plan Paper No. 1 had approved formation of an Air Arm for the Indian Navy, providing for the acquisition of two aircraft carriers with 46 carrier-borne aircraft to start naval aviation in the Indian Navy. But before this could be done, we needed to acquire aircraft carriers—ships that would act as vehicles for the plans in the high seas.

The first aircraft carrier that India considered acquiring was the HMS *Hercules*, a majestic class light fleet aircraft carrier.[2] In 1946, she was 75 per cent constructed when the Royal Navy stopped further work. She remained incomplete and mothballed for 11 years when she was purchased by India in 1957. The Indian Navy ordered an extended refit and modernization of the ship. These included, among other things, an angled deck, a steam catapult and a modified island. The work, undertaken at Harland and Wolff Shipyard in Belfast, Northern Ireland, took four years and was completed in 1961.

The Government of India set up an Internal Nomenclature Committee to select a name for the new aircraft carrier of the Indian Navy. In meetings, starting from April 1958, the committee considered and recommended 'Vindhya', 'Someru', 'Himalaya', 'Everest', 'Kanchenjunga', 'Kailash', 'Nanga Parbat' and 'Amarnath' as possible names, but they did not find favour with the government. A fresh direction was issued to the committee on 4 February 1959, and finally, 'Vikrant' was the name chosen for the first aircraft carrier of India. The ship was commissioned on 16 February 1961 as INS *Vikrant* on completion of her refit at Belfast.

The *Vikrant* displaced 19,500 tons at deep load. She had an overall length of 700 ft, a beam of 128 ft and a mean deep draught of 24 ft. She was powered by a pair of Parsons-geared

---

[2] In 1941, the UK ordered eight new aircraft carriers for the Royal Navy. As they were needed immediately, their specifications were simplified to cut the time and manufacture cost. Their planned operational life was just three years of active service. To reduce their manufacturing time, they were to be manufactured with the then existing power plants. These ships were given a special designation of majestic-class light fleet aircraft carriers.

steam turbine engines, driving two propeller shafts, using steam provided by four admiralty three-drum boilers. The turbines developed a total of 40,000 indicated horsepower, which gave a maximum speed of 25 knots or 46 km/hr. The air and ship crew comprised 1,110 officers and men.

INS *Vikrant* was armed with 16 40-mm Bofors anti-aircraft guns, but these were later reduced to eight. The ship was equipped with an air-search radar, a surface-search radar, a tactical radar and an aircraft landing radar, along with other communication systems.

The motto of INS *Vikrant* was: जयेमसंयुधिस्पृध, meaning 'I defeat those who fight against me'.

Rear Admiral S.K. Gupta, who was then part of the INAS 300 Squadron as one of the pilots, joined the Joint Services Wing (JSW) of the National Defence Academy (NDA) in Dehradun in July 1953 as a naval cadet. Midway through his three-year course, the JSW shifted to Khadakwasla, Pune. He joined the cadets training ship INS *Kistna* in June 1956, followed by INS *Tir* as a midshipman in 1957. When news spread of the intended acquisition of an aircraft carrier after Mountbatten's visit for one of the parades at the NDA, he joined the IAF Academy in Jodhpur the following year, flying the basic trainer HT-2, followed by the Texan T6G at the intermediate stage. He was found suitable to fly solo on the second day after a two-sortie check.

The naval pilots from the IAF selected for the fighter stream proceeded to Hakimpet, Secunderabad, for advanced flying of Vampires for one year. They were nine in number. On completion of flying training, they were certified fit to fly an aircraft and awarded 'Wings', which they could wear on their uniforms. They then joined INS Garuda, the naval air station at Cochin, in mid-1959. There, Rear Admiral S.K. Gupta converted to Sealand amphibious aircraft. Early next year, pilots were selected to proceed to the UK for fighter flying, while others for anti-submarine and recce flying went to Hyères, a naval facility in South of France.

Rear Admiral S.K. Gupta joined Naval Air Station (NAS), Brawdy, just prior to the commissioning of the squadron on 7 July 1960. HMS *Hercules* was renamed INS *Vikrant*. On that occasion, Rear Admiral, along with other pilots, did a fly-past with nine Sea Hawks over the ship from Brawdy. In return, Vijaya Lakshmi Pandit, the then India's High Commissioner in the UK, invited them in their flying overalls with various VIPs for a lunch on board INS *Vikrant*.

For the next one year, we received an intensive, interesting and challenging 'fighter' aircraft flying training at the Naval Air Station (NAS) Brawdy, in the UK. It was often in adverse flying conditions, so as to stay ahead of the ship's progress. So, when called upon, with the carrier now ready to receive the Sea Hawks, the pilots soon qualified on deck in August 1961. Soon, they learnt that in the Royal Navy parlance, it was a crime to keep the ship waiting and even on the first and only occasion, one had to explain in writing the cause of the delay.

The *Vikrant* finally sailed to the Mediterranean Sea to embark the Alizé aircraft of the Cobra squadron. This was followed by an intensive workup of the ship and her squadrons for a month off France, and then off the island of Malta until the end of October 1961. With *Vikrant* and her squadrons now fully operational, the ship sailed for home to Bombay but not before a formal goodwill VIP visit to Alexandria, Egypt. It was evident that there existed a special affinity between Pandit Nehru and Egypt's President Gamal Abdel Nasser. Finally, with the PM on board on 3 November 1961, the *Vikrant* docked in Bombay at the commercial docks. On 11 November 1961, the Sea Hawk squadron flew out to Sulur, Coimbatore.

This was an IAF depot for keeping their aircraft in storage until required. This was also to become the airfield for continuation flying for the White Tigers squadron for the next three years. The entire crew was accommodated within the IAF premises in Coimbatore, while INS Garuda, in Cochin, became the home for

Alizé or King Cobra squadron INAS 310, whenever the *Vikrant* was under dockyard maintenance in Bombay. At first, conditions were rudimentary in Coimbatore, both for aircraft maintenance and for ground and aircrew accommodation, until the commissioning of INS Hansa in early 1964. The Hansa shifted to its permanent location in Dabolim, Goa, in 1964. The Cobra squadron too moved to Goa in the mid-seventies.

The *Vikrant* sailed from Belfast on 5 March 1961 for sea trials. Capt. Pritam Singh Mahindroo was the commanding officer, Cdr Y.N. Singh was the commander (air), and Cdr Gautam Singh was the executive officer. Lt Cdr Balbir Dutt Law was the lieutenant commander (flying). The *Vikrant* conducted the sea trials of all her equipment for a month and then returned to Belfast for rectification of defects and the final testing and tuning. Lt Cdr R.H. Tahiliani carried out the first deck landing of a Sea Hawk on 18 May 1961, and five days later, the first Alizé plane landed on the *Vikrant* on 23 May 1961. The *Vikrant* was ready to leave the UK and proceed to India by June 1961. She sailed from Belfast in June-end 1961 and embarked the Sea Hawks of the new 300 Squadron on 4 August 1961 in Portsmouth, England.

The ship then left Portsmouth for Toulon at the end of June 1961, where the Alizés embarked the ship. With them on board, the *Vikrant* sailed in July 1961 for the Mediterranean region around Malta for operational training and workup. It was an intense flying phase when the *Vikrant* carried out nearly 1,000 catapult launches and deck landings. It proved that the *Vikrant* and her squadrons had achieved a high standard of professional proficiency. INS *Vikrant* then left the Mediterranean Sea and arrived in India via the Suez Canal, along with her squadrons of Sea Hawks and Alizés to a rousing welcome by the nation. It was a proud moment for the *Vikrant* and all those who had worked hard to realize the Indian dream of being the first in the South Asian region to operate an aircraft carrier.

More Ships Bought from the UK

The purchase of the second aircraft carrier, though approved in the Plan Paper No. 1 of 1948, was not pursued in the 1950s due to budget constraints. The Indian Navy purchased the second aircraft carrier, INS *Viraat*, from the UK in 1987, 30 years after the purchase of the *Vikrant*.

Continuing with the implementation of the approval of the Plan Paper No. 1, the first capital ship to be acquired from the UK in 1948 was a Leander-class light cruiser built for the Royal Navy in 1933 called HMS *Achilles*. During the Second World War, she had taken part in the Battle of the River Plate, close to the coast of Uruguay and Argentina in South America, as part of the Royal Navy ships hunting the German battleship *Graf Spee*. India purchased the *Achilles* in 1948 and recommissioned her as HMIS *Delhi* in London under the command of Capt. H.N.S. Brown, a Royal Navy officer. She was 14 years old at the time. Besides Capt. Brown, she had 17 British officers and senior sailors in the commissioning crew. Cdr Ram, the seniormost Indian officer in the RIN at the time, was her executive officer, and Lt Sardarilal Mathradas Nanda was her first lieutenant. Later, both of them were to become the CNS. In 1950, on India becoming a republic, she was renamed INS Delhi, and in June 1950, Cdr (later CNS) Adhar Kumar Chatterji became her first Indian commanding officer.

The second capital ship to be acquired by the Indian Navy was the 10,450-ton Fiji-class cruiser. She was built in the UK in 1939 as HMS *Nigeria*. She had served in the Second World War. She was purchased by the Indian Navy in August 1957 and recommissioned as INS *Mysore*. She had four propeller shafts, maximum speed of 33 knots (61 km/hr), along with 907 officers and men. She was in service in the Indian Navy for 28 years and was decommissioned in 1985.

Apart from these ships and INS *Vikrant*, the Indian Navy purchased the second aircraft carrier from the UK in 1987—

the erstwhile HMS *Hermes* of the British Royal Navy. She was launched in 1953 and commissioned into the Royal Navy in November 1959. She saw action in the 10-week undeclared war between Argentina and the UK in 1982 over the Falkland Islands, a British-dependent territory in the South Atlantic region. The Royal Navy decommissioned HMS *Hermes* in 1984. India purchased her and she was commissioned into the Indian Navy on 12 May 1987 as INS *Viraat* after a major refit in the UK. She was the last British-built ship to serve with the Indian Navy and was the oldest aircraft carrier in service in the world. The Indian Navy decommissioned the *Viraat* on 6 March 2017 after it completed nearly 30 years of service.

≈

4

Indian Naval Aviation Takes Off

Even as these ships were being acquired, the aviation arm of the Indian Navy was coming together. Its development had begun even before Independence.

The RIN had deputed one of its officers, Lt (later commodore) Y.N. Singh, to the UK in 1941 for basic flying training. He was later deputed to Canada, where he was awarded 'Wings', which he could wear on his uniform, signifying that he was a qualified pilot, before serving in escort carriers of the Royal Navy during the War. He was the first Indian naval pilot. He was later transferred from the British Royal Navy to the Indian Navy. He served as director of the naval air staff and retired in 1967 as commodore.

Planning an Aviation Arm

Despite Plan Paper No. 1 having provisions for naval aviation, the Royal Navy expressed its inability to spare any naval aircraft for transfer to the Indian Navy at that time. It was decided to look elsewhere for the aircraft, and to set up a shore-based nucleus of a naval aviation unit when these were acquired, with the added provision for future expansion. This requirement was included in the Defence Budget for 1949–50. Decisions were also taken to acquire the first aircraft carrier by 1955, the second two years later, and 300 fighter and anti-submarine aircraft by 1957. Out of these aircraft, 54 were to be carrier-borne and the rest were to be used ashore as trainers and reserves, and for shore-based operations. The British-manufactured Sea Fury FB 11 was selected as the primary shore-based strike aircraft, with 40 aircraft to be procured by 1950. Around this time, international events like the Berlin blockade and the war in Korea began to cast their shadows on the acquisition plans of the Indian Navy. The changed international situation altered the priorities of the major naval powers and an element of uncertainty was introduced in the availability of ships and aircraft for the Indian Navy's Air Arm. The Government of India took steps to resolve these issues.

The most critical problem was the shortage of trained and skilled officers and men. Thirteen officers were selected in 1948 for preliminary flying aptitude screening. They reported to the IAF station at Jodhpur in January 1949 for flying training. Out of these, 10 officers qualified and were selected for training with the Royal Navy in the UK. These were: Lieutenants H.K. Mukherji, A.S. Bathena, K. Cockburn, M.M. Bakshi, R.S. Sokhi, P. Parashar, T. Chakraverti, P.C. Rajkhowa, G.C.D. Cruz and B.D. Law. They left for the UK for preliminary flying training at Royal Naval Air Station Donibristle in Scotland. Three dropped out while seven completed the training successfully. They proceeded to the Royal Air Force (RAF) Syerston for further training, where five were declared successful and awarded 'Wings' on 13 July 1950.

These five were the first naval pilots of the Indian naval aviation. Based on their flying performance and overall assessment, the Royal Navy also decided who among the successful five would be the fighter pilots and who would join the anti-submarine warfare stream. They were accordingly segregated and sent to RAF

Lossiemouth for operational training in their allotted stream. The final successful ones were Lt Madan Bakshi, Lt Tuhin Chakraverti and Lt Raghubir Sokhi for anti-submarine operations; and Balbir Dutt Law and Lt Pran Parashar were selected for fighter operations. During this training, Bakshi died in a crash of a Firefly aircraft during a low-level sortie, leaving four naval pilots: Sokhi, Parashar, Chakraverti and Law.

Parashar and Law were sent to the 781 Communications Squadron, and Sokhi and Chakraverti to the 771 Fleet Requirements Squadron at Lee-on-Solent for further training. The Government of India sanctioned the FAA of the Indian Navy on 13 November 1950. The proposal envisaged training of pilots for the Fleet Requirements Unit (FRU), initially in India and then in the UK. It also sanctioned the training of naval aviation observers, air traffic control officers, aircraft engineering officers and the sailors in different trades and specializations for the naval aviation at the Royal Navy's aviation and technical institutions.

At this stage, there was a reappraisal of the nation's finances, leading to budgetary constraints on all ongoing schemes and expenditure. This affected the navy's plan for all acquisitions, especially the newly sanctioned Air Arm. A decision was made to reduce the strength to a small carrier force, with the primary task of anti-submarine warfare to be developed around one aircraft carrier instead of the two envisaged earlier. A second review in September 1950 decided on the development of only an FRU for naval aviation with 12 aircraft. Indian Navy bought 12 Sealand amphibian aircraft under this sanction, to be delivered in 1953. Lt B.D. Law and Lt Pran Parashar stayed back in the UK for twin-engine aircraft and amphibian training. Lt Parashar returned to India by the end of 1952, while Lt Law stayed on in the UK for further training.

Lt Cdr G. Douglas, an Indian who was decorated during the Second World War as a commissioned officer with the Royal Navy's FAA, was granted permanent commission with the rank of lieutenant commander in the Indian Navy. In addition, Lt N. Pavamana, Lt C.R. Menon, Lt Joginder Singh and Lt B.R. Acharya, who had been training with the IAF, joined the Indian naval aviation on completion of their flying training.

A massive programme of selection and professional training of officers and sailors in the UK was set in motion. By the time the refitting of the *Vikrant* was completed, the officers had been trained for the Sea Hawk squadron named INAS 300, which was commissioned on 7 July 1960 at the RNAS Brawdy, Pembrokeshire.

The first three pilots of INAS 300 were Lt Cdr Balbir Dutt Law, Lt Cdr B.R. Acharya and Lt R.N. Ghosh. The officers deputed to the UK in December 1959 were Lt S.G. Vichare, the AEO, Lt K.N.G. Menon, the air electric officer, S.D. Singh, the chief aircraft artificer of the squadron, and 40 sailors for aircraft maintenance and other support operations.

In addition to the aircrew, the newly-sanctioned FAA needed qualified aircraft engineers. Two marine engineer officers of the navy, Lt (later commander) P.V. George and Lt Cdr (later rear admiral) H.D. Kapadia, were selected for conversion to naval aviation and sent to the UK for training and specialization. Two engineer officers of the IAF, Lt (later commander) M.S. Shrikhande and Lt (later commander) V.S.P. Mudaliar were transferred to the aviation wing of the Indian Navy to help establish the infrastructure for the new Air Arm.

Rear Admiral Kapadia had a long association with naval aviation and made significant contributions to the development and maintenance of manpower and support facilities, along with the creation of aircraft maintenance facilities and infrastructure.

In 1949, 25 engine room artificers from the marine engineering branch were also selected for conversion to naval aviation for aircraft maintenance and engineering duties, and deputed to the UK for the Aircraft Artificers' Conversion Course at the RNAS, Arbroath. In September 1950, a proposal to establish a School of Aircraft Maintenance at Cochin was considered but dropped. The proposal was revived and, on 3 June 1957, the Naval Air Technical School (NATS) was set up at Cochin, with Lt Commander V.V. Narayan as its first officer-in-charge, for providing training to all naval aviation technical personnel as well as pilots, observers and flight engineers.

Until 1956, maintenance of all naval aircraft had been entrusted to Hindustan Aeronautics Limited (HAL), Bangalore, but in July 1956, the HAL set up a repair unit at Cochin. However, it was felt that the navy itself should undertake the maintenance of all its aircraft on its own. Hence, a Naval Aircraft Repair Organisation (NARO) was established at Cochin in February 1960 with Lt Cdr V.S.P. Mudaliar as its first superintendent. This organization was also entrusted with the testing and tuning of all new aircraft systems and equipment. The Naval Aircraft Inspection Service (later renamed as Naval Aircraft Quality Assurance Service) was established in November 1960, with Lt J. Stephen as its first chief inspection officer, for ensuring high standards of quality control of all systems and equipment fitted in naval aircraft. These organizations were modelled on the lines of similar infrastructure existing in the British Royal Navy in the UK for their naval aircraft. Capt. H.D. Kapadia became the director of Naval Air Material in January 1963.

Similarly, facilities were established in Bombay Naval Dockyard for the different levels of routine and deep maintenance of the aircraft carrier INS *Vikrant* and her equipment.

The Sea Hawk

Now that preparations had been made with trained officers, and an aircraft carrier had been acquired, the ship needed to be equipped with suitable aircraft to be able to fulfil its purpose. The Government of India selected the British-made Sea Hawk jet fighter aircraft as the main aircraft to operate from INS *Vikrant*.

Sea Hawks had been used by the Royal Navy as carrier-borne jet fighters and had proved themselves during the Suez Canal operations against Egypt on 31 October 1956.

The Sea Hawk was one of the first fixed-wing carrier-borne naval jet fighter aircraft of the world to come out after the Second World War. It was designed in the 1940s for carrier-borne fighter and ground attack roles. This was the time that saw the advent of the jet engine in place of the earlier four-stroke internal combustion engines of the automobile vehicles, which were modified to power the aircraft of late 1930s. The jet engine invented by Frank Whittle of the UK revolutionized both military and commercial aviation. It had the major advantages of being light weight as well as simple and reliable. The higher power-to-weight ratio of the jet engines was a distinct advantage when compared with the piston engine design—either two stroke or four stroke—of the engines used till then.

The design and development of the Sea Hawk took place in the final years of the Second World War. Its design was based on the then existing Hawker Sea Fury but was altered considerably in view of the experience gained during the War with fighter aircraft operations. The Sea Hawk was a single-seat aircraft. The cockpit was shifted to the front of the fuselage and the engine was fitted in the middle. The fuel tanks were installed in the centre of the aircraft, forward and aft of the engine, thereby helping to balance the centre of gravity of the aircraft. The aircraft had a maximum weight of 16,150 pounds and could achieve transonic speeds during dive. It had two forward looking 20-mm Hispano guns, a camera for photography and hard points under the wings to carry 500-pound bombs and 56-mm rockets. It could also carry two jettisonable fuel tanks under the wings for flying long distance.

The Sea Hawk was powered by a single, centre-line Rolls-Royce-Nene Mark 10,301 jet engine change unit. The jet exhaust from the engine discharged into two jet pipes, one on either side of the fuselage. The bifurcated jet exhaust was a brilliant design feature. It provided valuable additional space in the rear fuselage for a rear fuel tank, which permitted the aircraft to fly a longer range than many of the jet aircraft of that time. By doing away with a single centre-line exhaust pipe through the fuselage, the design provided space in the rear fuselage for aircraft controls, the hydraulic equipment for the arrestor hook operating system, and allowed storage of a small personal bag of the pilot when flying away from his base for short temporary duty.

The plane was coloured light blue in the upper half and white in the lower half. The undercarriage was of tricycle design rather than a tailwheel, which was the practice with the aircraft designers till then. This improved the range of vision of the pilot and made it easier to land on aircraft carriers. The oleo leg worked on the principle of liquid spring compression and decompression.

The Sea Hawk had a robust, reliable and elegant design. It incorporated the folding wing design to reduce its parking space for carrier operations. It was also fitted with an arrestor hook at the rear for recovery on the aircraft carrier's flight deck. It was a beautiful aircraft, especially when it was in flight. It was designed to carry out three roles—as fighter, for ground attack with rockets and cannons, and as a bomber.

A typical sortie of the aircraft was of about 35–50 minutes. It had the provision to carry two jettisonable fuel tanks, one under each wing, which increased its endurance to about 1 hour 20 minutes. It was not fitted with a radar—this was one of its major shortcomings. It could not operate at night or in poor visibility conditions. It was unable to locate targets at sea outside the visual range and had to be guided to the target. It was superseded by newer and more advanced carrier-based aircraft. The Royal Navy began to phase these out from frontline service in 1958. The last frontline Sea Hawk aircraft squadron of the Royal Navy was disbanded in December 1960.

Armstrong Whitworth, the manufacturers of Sea Hawks, had built a total of 542 Sea Hawks between September 1947 and July

1961. They were flown by the UK, German and Dutch navies, and also the Indian Navy. Each of these operators, except the Indian Navy, purchased new Sea Hawks and flew them for about seven years, and then withdrew them from service to replace them with more modern aircraft having better performance, ease of operation, improved structural design, engines, systems and equipment fit.

The Indian Navy eventually acquired 74 Sea Hawks in six batches; nine in 1959–60, 14 in 1961, seven in 1960–61, 10 in 1963, six again in 1963 and finally 28 in 1966. All the aircraft were purchased second-hand except the second batch, in which all 14 were bought new. Capt. R.H.P. Carver[1], CONA at the naval headquarters at the time, had projected a requirement of 23 Sea Hawks for INS *Vikrant*. The first batch of nine Sea Hawks was delivered to INAS 300 in the UK, commencing from December 1959. Of the new aircraft, two were delivered in the UK in January 1961 to INAS 300 at Royal Naval Air Station Brawdy, UK. The next three joined INAS 300 in the UK before the *Vikrant* left England on 7 August 1961 for her workup at Malta in Mediterranean Sea. Eight Sea Hawks joined the *Vikrant* when she was exercising at Malta. The last Sea Hawk of the second batch embarked the *Vikrant* at Malta on 4 October 1961. On completion of eight weeks of exercises and armament workup at Malta, the *Vikrant* set sail on 6 October 1961 for India via Suez Canal. These 23 Sea Hawks were on board INS *Vikrant* when she arrived in Bombay.

Launch from Anchorage

After the *Vikrant's* arrival in India from the UK on 3 November 1961, it was deployed in Operation Vijay on 15 December 1961,

---

[1]Captain R.H.P. Carver RN was one of the Royal Navy officers on loan to Indian Navy. He served as CONA at the naval headquarters from 27 August 1956 to 2 February 1959.

in which the Indian armed forces liberated Goa from Portuguese occupation. After the Liberation, the 300 Squadron of Sea Hawks disembarked from the *Vikrant* on 11 January 1962 and flew to Sulur. The Alizés of the 310 Squadron were also disembarked, and they flew to their base at Cochin. Two Sea Hawks, however, became unserviceable during the launch. The engineers of the squadron rectified the defects, but by then, the ship had called off the flying operations and had entered the Bombay harbour. It was scheduled to dry dock at the Naval Dockyard in Bombay the following morning. It was in this situation that the flying qualities of the Sea Hawk got tested unwittingly. It involved a highly unusual demand for two Sea Hawks and their pilots, when they were asked to launch by catapult from INS *Vikrant*, when the ship was stationary at anchorage in Bombay harbour. The launch from an anchored and non-moving aircraft carrier was neither authorized in any instruction manual nor had it ever been tried or put into practice in the Royal Navy or elsewhere, not even by the Indian Navy pilots when they were undergoing flying training. This is because planes on board aircraft carriers don't have runways, so they require the speed of the moving ship to take off. Stationary ships usually don't provide sufficient momentum for the plane to gain the necessary speed to take off.

On the eve of the *Vikrant*'s dry-docking, the two Sea Hawks left behind on board were now serviceable, but there was no way the *Vikrant* could sail out to the sea the next morning to launch the two aircraft and then return to harbour and proceed to dry dock. After hectic consultations, it was decided to launch the two Sea Hawks the following morning from the anchorage itself. The next morning, Lt (later rear admiral) Ranvijay Singh was launched first, and followed by Lt (later rear admiral) S.K. Gupta a few minutes later.

The *Vikrant* was at her usual berth at the naval anchorage in Bombay. Four of the Bombay Port Trust and naval tugs were following orders from the bridge where the commanding officer, Capt. P.S. Mahindroo, Cdr (Air) Y.N. Singh and the *Vikrant*'s Executive Officer Cdr Gautam Singh were present. Lt R.H. Tahiliani, the commanding officer of INAS 300, was on the flight deck, monitoring the launch. He had just taken over the squadron. Lt Cdr B.D. Law, the lieutenant commander (flying), was to conduct the launch, and Lt Cdr Acharya who was ready to take over as Little F[2] from him was present with him. Lt S.G. Vichare, the squadron AEO, and Lt C.K. Vishwanath, the squadron air electrical officer (ALO), were on the flight deck with the squadron air engineering sailors, supervising the preparation of the aircraft for the launch. The other heads of the departments who were monitoring the event were Cdr Rajan, the ship's AEO; Lt Cdr Madholkar, the ship's ALO; Lt Cdr Puri, the flight deck officer; Lt Cdr Bilu Chaudhuri, the flight deck engineer officer; Cdr (E) Edwards, ship's engineer officer; and Cdr (L) P.K. Sinha, ship's electrical officer.

'There must have been other naval ships at anchorage but I do not recall that,' says Rear Admiral Gupta. The Western Naval Command had detailed one of the Rajput-class destroyers as the plane guard ship. One Alouette helicopter of the *Vikrant* was airborne to provide the search and rescue (SAR) cover as per the standard operating procedure.

The launch of the Sea Hawks was to be in the westerly direction to take advantage of the oncoming sea breeze. However, the ship lay broadside into wind in the northerly direction, as it was difficult to move the ship into the wind and then hold it there. Rear Admiral Gupta says, 'If I can remember correctly, I am certain the FOB [Flag Officer Bombay], FOCIF [Flag Officer Commanding Indian Fleet] would have been informed of the launch of two Sea Hawks by the *Vikrant* in the harbour and from anchorage. So, I assume it was the decision of the Commanding Officer of INS *Vikrant*.'

---

[2]On the aircraft carrier, lieutenant commander (flying) was also called Little F.

The carrier had to make it back to the harbour for docking the next morning and the aircraft had to be disembarked before the ship's movement for docking. The choice lay in disembarking them alongside the jetty and then towing them 30 km by tractor by the city roads at midnight to Santa Cruz airport. The other alternative was to fly them off the carrier from anchorage. Since the ship's docking plans could not be postponed, it was decided to launch the two Sea Hawks by the ship's catapult at anchorage. The winds were marginal, and the ship was turned into the wind with the help of tugs. The aircraft were defueled with minimum fuel to reduce their weight for a short flight from anchorage to Santa Cruz.

After various attempts in holding the ship into the wind by tugs, the first Sea Hawk was catapult-launched in marginal conditions, and was seen to sink somewhat. The ship's engineers adjusted the steam pressure for the catapult and, a few minutes later, the second Sea Hawk was launched with a bigger punch from the catapult. The second launch was clean. Five minutes later, both the aircraft landed at the commercial airport in Santa Cruz for refuelling and to take off in formation for Goa, the home base. 'I am sure the sudden launch of two jet fighters roaring away from the *Vikrant* at anchorage would have been the surprise of a lifetime for the other naval and merchant ships at anchorage in the Bombay harbour, as well as the citizens of Bombay who saw the event that morning, as they would never witness a similar event again,' recalls Rear Admiral Gupta. This procedure of launching Sea Hawks from the *Vikrant* at anchorage was never attempted again.

Rear Admiral Gupta also participated in the Sea Hawk trials after the *Vikrant* had undergone its refit in Bombay. He recalls his experience of another unusual incident.

> In 1966, the Vikrant had just completed her dockyard refit at Bombay. She now needed to carry out the post-refit flying trials at sea to test its systems by operating aircraft. Since

INAS 300 and her Sea Hawk aircraft were based at Goa, the ship sailed from Bombay to Goa to carry out the mandatory aircraft flying trials from the ship at sea off Goa. The trials procedure involved a couple of engagements on each wire pull-out by the aircraft on recovery. The arrester assembly was then inspected by the flight deck engineer officer and his team. The pilots selected were the most experienced on carrying out deck operations. I was chosen to carry out the trials for the Sea Hawk aircraft. I took off in a Sea Hawk and on my first attempt, the aircraft plucked/engaged the target wire no. 3, as the approach and hitting the deck with right speed and attitude was correct. I felt some retardation, but thought that it was only momentary. So without hesitation, I applied full power to get airborne. There was a noticeable sinking of the aircraft after rolling off the deck, with the ship's flying control (FLYCO) warning on radio transmission. I did, for a brief second, consider ejecting from the Sea Hawk, just when the aircraft picked up flying speed. I was diverted to Dabolim. On landing and inspecting the aircraft with the ground crew, we observed that the entire hook assembly was missing. We later learnt that the arrester wire had parted and rolled itself around the aircraft arrestor hook assembly, wrenching it off the aircraft! A major accident had been averted.

Ferry Flight of Two Aircraft

The 23 Sea Hawks of the third, fourth and fifth batches were used, ex-Royal Navy aircraft. They were ferry flown to India—meaning they were flown with the express purpose of delivery—between October 1962 and February 1965.

Rear Admiral S.K. Gupta narrates his experience of ferrying two Sea Hawks from the UK to India. Ten Sea Hawks were ferried from Belfast to Sulur, the Indian base in Coimbatore, by the 300 Squadron pilots, saving valuable foreign exchange for the country, as shipping didn't need to be paid for. This allowed the pilots to experience ferry hopping through several countries, and inspecting the aircraft after (AFI—after flight inspection) and before every flight (BFI—before flight inspection). No back-up, multi-engine support aircraft was to accompany the ferries. The Sea Hawks were ferried from the UK to India in three separate ferries. 'The third ferry in February 1963 was of two Sea Hawks by Tippy [Lt Tipnis] and myself,' says Rear Admiral Gupta.

After test flying and acceptance of the Sea Hawks, the duo routed themselves as follows: (Sydenham) Belfast–Orange–Napoli–Hal Far (Malta)–El Adam–Cairo–Beirut–Baghdad–Bahrain–Sharjah–Karachi–Bombay–Sulur (Coimbatore). The ferry took five days longer than planned, owing to aircraft cartridge-starter defects in Orange, Beirut and at RAF Sharjah.

At Sharjah, the pilots arrived at the RAF officers' mess at night. There was a social evening and they got an invitation. They had no clothes other than one set of the usual evening shirt and tie, and a pair of trousers, so they excused themselves, and having had a long day, they went to bed. There was a loud banging on the door, and they were persuaded to attend since it was an informal evening with everyone donning their Arabian dress. The excuse that they would be inappropriately dressed was not accepted, as by now the party was in full swing.

'This is how we both dressed for the party,' recalls Rear Admiral Gupta. 'For the head dress, we placed our white pillow covers over our head and tied them with our ties to hold them in place. Over the shirt and trouser, we each tied the bedsheet around us with a belt to keep it in place. We then joined the party! We were instant hits with both officers and their ladies. It must have been either because we looked comical, or they appreciated that we were good sports to have joined in.' There was dancing, and after a couple of much-needed drinks, they found the floor. It was a very enjoyable evening.

They did not take off the next morning, as they were both not fit for two long flights. Luck was with them, as there was a delay of two more days, for one of the aircraft had become unserviceable. The RAF replaced it with a new one flown from the UK, and thus the ferry continued.

The flight from Sharjah to Karachi was over 600 nautical miles. They arrived there with little fuel. Since relations between the two countries were sour, at Karachi, they had to fuel the aircraft and obtain take-off clearance after the aircraft had been fumigated. The onward flight to Bombay was uneventful. However, after fuelling the aircraft at Bombay to take off for Coimbatore, the home base, they were confronted by the Customs. They had to spend over two hours explaining that the aircraft were military planes of the Indian Navy, hence not dutiable. The Customs officials were not sure if the pilots had tape recorders hidden in the aircraft somewhere. They offered to take their inspectors to the planes. The issue was resolved with the arrival of authorization from the navy to fly the two Sea Hawks to Coimbatore. 'We concluded that our flight plan had not been communicated to the navy from Bombay authorities, hence the delay in the arrival of the naval personnel with proper authorization,' says Rear Admiral Gupta.

The German Sea Hawks

The German Navy had started its FAA in 1958–59 with 68 new Sea Hawks purchased from the UK. They began their flying operations in July 1958 and were retired seven years later in 1965. The Indian Navy approached the German Navy to purchase 28 of these German Sea Hawks on an 'as is where is' basis. Commodore George Douglas was the CONA, and Capt. P.V. George was the director of Naval Material at the naval headquarters at the time.

Capt. George was deputed to visit Germany on 18 August 1965 to hold discussions and price negotiations. The finalized package included 28 used German Sea Hawks, 40 spare Nene engines, 104 guns, ammunition and other spares, for which a price of ₹52 lakh was agreed upon. It was a windfall deal. If we consider ₹52.5 lakh as the cost of 28 Sea Hawks and the balance ₹10 lakh as the cost of 40 spare Nene engines, 104 aircraft guns and other spares, the cost of each Sea Hawk jet fighter works out to be only ₹1.5 lakh.[3] Compared to this, the 23 Sea Hawks of the first and second batches purchased about six years earlier had cost Indian Navy ₹200.48 lakh. The average cost per Sea Hawk paid in 1960–61 works out to ₹8.72 lakh. The deal was, therefore, at least six times cheaper. If we consider that the Sea Hawks, their engines and their equipment fit were not manufactured any more, the value of the deal becomes more attractive.

Lt Cdr B.K. Malik and chief aircraft artificer Babu were deputed to West Germany in mid-June 1966 to organize shipping of the consignment to India. The aircraft and the equipment were in a knocked down state and had been packed in 40-foot-long wooden crates. The Government of India had hired a merchant ship for the purpose, and the consignment was loaded onto the ship in June-end 1966. The ship, with Lt Cdr Malik and chief aircraft artificer Babu also on board, sailed from the German seaport Bremen for India and arrived in Cochin on 23 July 1966. The remaining parts were delivered to India by sea later.

The aircraft were assembled at NARO, located at INS Garuda, Cochin. Cdr Joginder Singh was the superintendent at the time. All the German Sea Hawks were subjected to detailed inspection for their fitness and airworthiness after assembly. The quality of the work was overseen and certified by the Naval Aircraft Inspection Service as per the laid down instructions. On completion, they were test flown by Indian pilots for final certification and clearance to enter frontline squadron service with the Indian Navy.

---

[3] Pasricha, Vinod, *Downwind, Four Green*, Pashmira Publications, 2010, p. 57, 148.

Naresh Kumar Vohra, who was a young aircraft artificer at the time and involved in this important work at NARO, Cochin, said:

> In May 1966, I was an Aircraft Artificer 4, serving in the Sea Hawk hangar of NARO. I was part of a team of six formed to assemble the German Sea Hawks and carry out maintenance check to make them airworthy for frontline squadron service. It was a complex and specialized work never done before and we were proud to have been chosen for it. The wings were packed in separate crates. The engines were sealed in heavy plastic covers and crated, to prevent ingress of moisture during sea passage. All packaging was of the highest standard, and when opened, the parts inside were in sound and preserved condition; there was no evidence of any corrosion of the parts. The aircraft instruments, accessories, ejection seats, fuel drop tanks and such other items were packed in separate crates and listed.
>
> The aircraft documents and the logbooks of each aircraft were stowed in the cockpit of that aircraft. All documents were up to date and maintained meticulously.
>
> Kirpal Singh, chief aircraft artificer [CAA], Mr George, civilian group leader, and Mr Baby, civilian aircraft fitter, were other members of the assembly team. CAA C.J. Rana looked after the inspections and CAA P.K. Rawat handled the documentation. All the 28 Sea Hawk aircraft were assembled, test flown and certified airworthy within a year of their arrival.
>
> The 28 German Sea Hawks helped the Indian Navy to maintain an effective availability of aircraft for the frontline flying operations. In 1971, a frontline aircraft establishment of 18 Sea Hawks were allotted to INAS 300 jet fighter squadron, which embarked on the *Vikrant* and went to war. Out of these, five were from the ex-UK supply, and the

remaining 13 were from the old and used aircraft purchased from Germany.

Alizé: French Anti-Submarine Aircraft

Along with the squadron INS 300 of the Sea Hawks, a squadron of French anti-submarine, turboprop, Alizé aircraft was also purchased for the *Vikrant*.

Alizé was a French carrier-based anti-submarine warfare (ASW) aircraft developed in the 1950s. It was a low-wing monoplane of conventional configuration powered by a single Rolls-Royce Dart turboprop engine. It outdid the Sea Hawk in that it had a radar system with a retractable antenna dome in its belly. The cockpit accommodated a crew of three, including the pilot, radar operator and sensor operator, as opposed to the single-seater Sea Hawk. The pilot was seated in front on the left, the navigator in front on the right and the sensor operator sat sideways behind them. It had an arresting hook for carrier-borne operations. The internal weapons bay could accommodate a homing torpedo, and underwing stores pylons could carry rockets, which allowed these planes to be effective for ASW.

In the summer of 1960, the Indian Navy deputed two pilots to France to train for flying Alizé. They became flying instructors to train and convert pilots who arrived from India later to join the Alizé squadron operating in France.

INAS 310, the anti-submarine squadron of the Indian Navy, was commissioned in France on 21 March 1961 by Nawab Ali Yavar Jung Bahadur, the then Ambassador of India to France. The squadron was to fly the French manufactured Alizé aircraft for carrier operations. The Alizé anti-submarine, turboprop aircraft manufactured by Breguet of France, was the choice for the *Vikrant*. Although its ASW capability was relatively modest, the Indian Navy's choice of Alizé as an aviation services management platform aircraft was a well thought out decision.

The Indian Navy signed a deal with France in 1960 to procure 12 aircraft and raised INAS 310 to receive them. Admiral R.D. Katari, the CNS of the Indian Navy, visited the manufacturers of Alizé aircraft in France on 28 October 1960 to witness a flight demonstration of Alizé. The first Alizé, IN 201, was handed over to the Indian Navy at a ceremony in France on 7 January 1961.

The Indian naval induction team, comprising four aircrew members led by Lt Cdr M.K. Roy, squadron Cdr-designate, first arrived at Hyères in France on 28 September 1960 for testing, trials and acceptance of the Alizé aircraft. Lt Cdr Roy was appointed the first commanding officer of INAS 310 on 21 March 1961. From the next day, the Indian pilots carried out catapult-launches and deck landings on French aircraft carrier *Arromanches*. On 23 May 1961, Lt Raj Anderson and Lt Cdr Roy carried out the first deck landing of an Indian Alizé aircraft on board INS *Vikrant*, off Yeovilton in the UK.

INAS 310 was initially stationed at INS Garuda, Cochin. Later, the navy operated the Alizés from shore bases and from INS *Vikrant*. The Alizé aircraft saw their first action in December 1961 as the squadron flew sorties for anti-submarine patrols and reconnaissance missions for Operation Vijay.

During the Indo-Pak War of 1965, the Alizé aircraft was in action again when they operated in two detachments from Bombay and Cochin. They were tasked to defend their own fleet at Bombay and Cochin harbours, and aid in the destruction of the enemy ships. In addition, one aircraft was tasked to undertake operations for electronic surveillance measures along the western borders of India from Jamnagar to Pathankot.

The Indian Navy purchased two Alizés in addition to the initial 12 in 1968. In April 1970, the squadron shifted base from Cochin to Goa, and made significant contributions to the 1971 war. On 10 May 1987, after rendering 26 years of meritorious service on board INS *Vikrant*, the Alizé aircraft were finally disembarked. The Indian Navy phased out Alizés in 1991.

French Alouette Helicopters

A helicopter is an essential component of carrier operations. It is used for various purposes like SAR operations when a plane guard is not available. It can also be deployed for reconnaissance, ASW, and anti-ship operations using torpedoes and short-range missiles. When the acquisition of the *Vikrant* was finalized, the requirement of helicopters for the FAA was projected to the French naval authorities and, after the conversion of Lt Cdr P.K.K. Menon to helicopter-flying at IAF Station, Palam, two pilots, Lt M.P. Wadhawan and Lt (later commander) A.S. Dhillon were deputed to France in January 1961, for conversion to Alouette II helicopters. These helicopters were assessed superior to the British Dragonfly helicopters offered by the UK. Therefore, for the SAR operation, India opted for the single-jet engine French Alouette helicopters.

The Alouette II was cheaper and powered by a gas turbine engine. With it, there was no need to store petrol on board the ship, as was the case with the helicopters offered by the UK. The French Navy provided two Alouette II helicopters to Indian Navy on loan for three months. They were returned after the Indian pilots had been trained in SAR operations. Finally, the Indian Navy opted for Alouette III helicopters from Sud Aviation, France. The first two helicopters arrived at Santa Cruz, Bombay, in mid-1964, in crates. These were assembled by the navy's air engineers with the assistance of a French technician and numbered IN 131 and IN 132. They were test flown in Bombay and then flown to the east coast to join INS *Vikrant*. They embarked on the *Vikrant* on 11 July 1964.

Later HAL, Bangalore, began to manufacture them as Chetaks under license from its French manufacturer, Sud Aviation. On the

Indian Navy's request, HAL modified the Chetak to play the role of medium-range, anti-submarine torpedo-carrying helicopter. In its new role, this helicopter was called by its acronym MATCH, and was equipped with anti-submarine weapons comprising two depth-charges or two anti-submarine torpedoes, or a mix of the two. MATCH was taken in for operating from the *Vikrant* and tankers, frigates, destroyers and even survey ships. This versatile workhorse, known for its ease of flying and maintenance, has an unmatched record of aircraft safety and has served the Indian Navy for nearly 60 years. On 14 March 1969, all the Chetak flights of the Indian Navy were merged to form one squadron, named INAS 321. Some prominent names among the pioneering pilots of Alouettes and Chetaks in the Indian naval aviation are Lieutenant(s) M.P. Wadhawan, V. Ravindranath, Chief D.K. Yadav, S.R. Debgupta, A.S. Dhillon, H.M. Gori, Piyush Jha and D.S. Mokha.

Equipped with folding blades, Chetak was powered by an 8,700-shaft-horsepower jet turbine engine. It had an endurance of 2.5 hours, with a maximum speed of 113 knots. It had a crew of three—a pilot, a co-pilot and an aircrew—for undertaking rescue operations at sea.

The three types of aircraft chosen for the *Vikrant*—the Sea Hawk fighter-ground attacker and bomber, the Alizé anti-submarine aircraft and the Alouette III helicopter—were able to perform all the roles of carrier-borne aircraft, such as air defence of the fleet; merchant shipping; maritime reconnaissance; anti-ship strike; anti-submarine defence; SAR; minelaying; ground attack; support of ground forces; aerial photography and the logistic role of transfer of personnel.

Acquisition of INS *Vikrant* and her aircraft squadrons of jet fighter Sea Hawks, anti-submarine aircraft Alizés and SAR French helicopters Alouettes marked the beginning of the real naval aviation in the Indian Navy. Then on, the Indian Navy worked hard to create an efficient network of skilled personnel, institutions and infrastructure needed for an efficient naval aviation. Thus, the basic support infrastructure for naval aviation had been established before INS *Vikrant* arrived in India on 3 November 1961. These were modelled on the skills and infrastructure available for the FAA of the Royal Navy in the UK. The establishment of an efficient naval aviation in the Indian Navy paid major dividends in 1971 and continues to do so.

This entire investment in the *Vikrant* paid off in the 1971 war, as we shall see. INS *Vikrant* was the star performer in the 1971 Indo-Pak War in the Bay of Bengal and crafted the Indian victory. It helped the Indian Navy in becoming the dominant regional power.

THE BELOVED SEA HAWK

Those who flew the Sea Hawk fell in love with the aircraft. They recall their association with it as a wonderful time, even after they have hung their boots and are now leading retired lives. One such fan is Rear Admiral Purushottam Dutt Sharma (Retd). Here he recalls his flying days with the Sea Hawk (as told to the authors).

My association with the Sea Hawk began on 20 September 1962, in Sulur near Coimbatore. I had barely flown for seven hours on it when I was asked to go for local flying sortie and aerobatics. I found myself trying to do a stall turn—an aerobatics turn-around manoeuvre—on the Sea Hawk. I had done those quite well on T6Gs earlier during training. That sortie on Sea Hawk over Stanley Reservoir off Mettur Dam near the foothills of Ooty was quite an experience! The aircraft was almost in a vertical climb, close to zero on the ASI [Air Speed Indicator], with full rudder trying to cartwheel the aircraft into a stall turn. It went into an unusual manoeuvre, which I could not understand.

Unhappy with the outcome of my first attempt, I climbed back to 15,000 ft and tried the same manoeuvre at a little higher speed with almost similar result. I realized the Sea Hawk was not meant to fly like a T6G. A few loops and barrel rolls later, I was back at the base only to be told that jets don't do stall turns. I accepted this, but today I see MIG 29s and Sukhoi 30s fly over my house in Pune doing similar manoeuvres with ease. I guess it is a question of the power-weight ratio of aircraft and, of course, the vectored thrust.

I had implicit faith in my AEOs, who were telling me that the aircraft I was to fly was good. I always took it up without a worry, and my Sea Hawk and I played together, often surprising each other. There were hydraulic or radio transmission failures galore, a few occasions of imbalance between front and rear fuel tanks, leading to manual balancing; there was a 'controls jammed' situation after a catapult launch, and even a saddle tank burst on the finals, forcing me to do a flapless to extend the glide to the runway! On one occasion, in 1965, we had the entire fleet firing at us as my Sea Hawk was silently limping back from Jamnagar to Bombay. But we survived due to some bad shooting or our joint good luck!

The crowning glory was our togetherness during the 1971 Indo-Pak conflict. I was on board the *Vikrant* as a guest from the naval headquarters to spend a few days together again after a break. Sea Hawk IN 173 and I were together on three occasions when the engine oil system surprised us with pressure showing zero on launch. But we pressed on completing the task given to us every time. Gurnam, our AEO, was rattled sometimes but wouldn't give up and got known famously for his 18 on 18 aircraft serviceability repeatedly during those ops.

Timeline

The path of setting up the facilities for naval aviation in the early years is described below:

- **1947:** India gains independence.
- **1948:** Plan Paper No. 1 put up to the government gets approved.
- **1947–57:** Surface ships are acquired from the UK. Shore facilities are created to remedy dislocation caused by the partition of navy in 1947. Only shore-based aircraft are acquired.
- **1948:** Directorate of Naval Aviation begins to function.
- **1948–49:** Indian Navy officers and sailors start going to the UK for training as pilots, observers and for technical training in aircraft maintenance.
- **1949:** Capt. H.C. Ranalds RN is appointed as the first CONA.
- **1951:** An FRU is formed to meet the Indian Navy requirement of aircraft targets for gunnery practice, radar tracking practice, radar and communication calibration and for aircrew training.
- **1953:** On 1 January 1953, airfield at Cochin is taken over from the Director General of Civil Aviation. The navy assumes responsibility of the operation from the Cochin airfield. It is renamed INS Garuda a few months later.
- **1953:** Ten amphibian Sealand aircraft are acquired and based at Cochin.
- **1953:** The FRU is commissioned on 1 March 1953 and INS Garuda is commissioned as the Indian Navy's first naval air station on 11 May 1953.
- **1955:** Sealand aircraft are found unsuitable for anti-aircraft

firing practice. Ten target-towing British naval Firefly aircraft are inducted between 1955 and 1958. The last five of these are equipped with 20-mm cannon and are capable of carrying rockets and bombs. They mark the advent of the weapon capability in the Air Arm of the Indian Navy.

- **1955:** The Government of India approves the acquisition of one aircraft carrier from the UK.

- **1956:** The School for Naval Airmen is opened in Cochin in August.

- **1956:** Three Hindustan Trainer (HT-2) aircraft made by HAL join FRU in October to facilitate continuation flying. This is in continuation of the basic flying training being imparted to navy pilots by the IAF since 1952.

- **1957:** Deal for the purchase of one aircraft carrier, *Vikrant*, along with two aircraft squadrons, is finalized. The *Vikrant* commences four years of extensive refit-cum-modernization in the UK. Almost all the electronic and electric equipment have to be replaced. The ship has to be fitted with an angled deck, a steam catapult and a mirror landing sight.

- **1957:** Naval Air Technical School is started at INS Garuda, Cochin, in June.

- **1957:** Since the *Vikrant* is set to operate jet aircraft, the pilots have to undergo conversion to jet aircraft flying. Three single-seat Vampire jet aircraft are acquired from HAL. One two-seater Vampire trainer is transferred from the IAF to the navy. Since INS Garuda's runway is not long enough to operate the Vampires, from September 1957 onwards, a naval jet flight begins operations from the longer airfield at Sulur near Coimbatore.

- **1959:** On 17 January, FRU becomes the first naval aviation squadron to be commissioned as INAS 550. It has 10 amphibian Sealands, 10 target-towing Firefly aircraft and three HT-2 trainer aircraft.

- **1960:** The naval jet flight at Sulur is designated as INAS 550 A, and tasked with the training of pilots for *Vikrant*'s Sea Hawk Squadron. The FRU at Cochin is designated as INAS 550 B.

- **1960:** NARO is started in Cochin in February 1960. Its task is to repair and overhaul airframe and major components. The overhaul of the aero-engines is to be undertaken by HAL and the IAF.

- **1960:** The Observer School is started at Cochin.

- **1960:** Naval Aircraft Inspection Service (NAIS) is started in Cochin in November.

- **1961:** On 1 September, the aviation unit at Sulur is commissioned as INAS 551. On 5 September 1961, the naval jet flight is merged with the Naval Rifle Range Detachment in Coimbatore and commissioned as INS Hansa.

- **1961:** INS *Vikrant*, the White Tigers and the Cobras arrive in Bombay from the UK on 3 November and are welcomed by PM Jawaharlal Nehru and Defence Minister V.K. Krishna Menon.

- **1962:** After the liberation of Goa in December 1961, the Indian Navy takes over the airfield at Dabolim, Goa, in April.

- **1964:** INS Hansa and INAS 551 are relocated from Coimbatore to Dabolim in June. In July, government sanction is accorded for Goa to be a full-fledged NAS, and to be equipped with Ground Control Approach (GCA) radar. In November, the Sea Hawk squadron INAS 300 disembarks from the *Vikrant* directly at Goa.

- **1964:** The Fireflies and the HT-2 trainer aircraft are retired.

- **1965:** The Sealand amphibian aircraft are retired.

- **1965–1971:** Regular embarkations of the squadrons on INS *Vikrant* for flying practice begin.

PART TWO

5

First Stirrings of War

At the time of Partition, India was divided into three parts: one was the Indian mainland, which became India; the second was the northwestern part of Punjab, which became West Pakistan; and third was the eastern part of Bengal, which became East Pakistan.

Tensions within Pakistan

In the late 1960s, the relations between the two wings of Pakistan—the eastern in the Bay of Bengal and the western in the Arabian Sea—had been deteriorating for a long time. With relations at a nadir, the differences between West Pakistan and East Pakistan became irreconcilable. From 1968, the internal problems of Pakistan headed for an internecine civil war between the people of West Pakistan and those of East Pakistan.

The intense feeling of discrimination in the minds of the Bengali-speaking population of East Pakistan had its roots in the formation of Pakistan itself. The first shock to the Bengalis had come when Mohammed Ali Jinnah, the first governor general of Pakistan, had declared in 1947—a few months after Pakistan had become an independent nation—that Urdu would be the sole national language of Pakistan, and the order would apply to everyone, including the Bengali-speaking people of East Pakistan. This had riled the people of East Pakistan, who were fiercely proud of their Bengali language, their literary heritage and their centuries-old culture. Urdu was a language totally alien to them. This sense of hurt had led to agitations and protests in East Pakistan, where people spoke and read only in Bengali, which was also the medium of instruction in schools and universities. From this fault line had begun the alienation of the two halves of Pakistan which, with the passage of years, became a deep corrosive fissure and ultimately broke the country in two.

West Pakistan was the seat of the Pakistani government and its population mainly consisted of Sindhis, Punjabis, Balochs and Pathans, who culturally, linguistically and traditionally had little in common with the Bengalis of East Pakistan. The only thing common between the two wings was Islam.

The period from the formation of Pakistan in 1947 to the late 1960s witnessed great economic disparity between East and West Pakistan. This was mainly the result of the subordination of the economic interests of the eastern wing. Further, East Pakistan generated much more revenue than West Pakistan from exports. The latter mopped up all this revenue but spent only a fraction of it on the development and welfare of the Bengalis of East Pakistan. Also, the West Pakistanis were appointed to most of the senior positions in the civilian administration and the armed forces, ignoring East Pakistanis and denying them employment and development opportunities. The East Pakistanis were sore about this brazen step-motherly treatment by the Pakistani government, and this deliberate discrimination bred even more resentment in the minds of the Bengali-speaking people of East Pakistan.

A local politician, Sheikh Mujibur Rahman, emerged as the organizer and leader of East Pakistanis in their struggle against their economic and cultural colonization by West Pakistan. To suppress this, the rulers in West Pakistan began a systematic policy of suppression of the people of East Pakistan. Sheikh Rahman was arrested in 1968, but due to his popularity among the masses, Ayub Khan, the president of Pakistan, had to set him free after two years. In March 1969, Pakistan came under martial law imposed by General Yahya Khan, who replaced Ayub Khan as the head of the government in a coup. Under one of the conditions of the martial law, Yahya Khan was obliged to hold general elections in Pakistan.

In January 1970, elections were announced. Yahya Khan had perhaps calculated that the general elections would not throw up a clear winner, and in the resulting stalemate, the armed forces would be able to manipulate the process and form a puppet government of their choice. The assumptions and calculations of Yahya Khan were proved wrong by the electorate.

East Pakistan gave an overwhelming mandate to Sheikh Mujibur Rahman. His Awami League Party won 167 of the 169 East Pakistan seats in the National Assembly. In the west, Zulfikar Ali Bhutto's Pakistan People's Party got two-thirds of the remaining 144 seats in the National Assembly. Sheikh Rahman had won an absolute majority and should have become the PM of Pakistan. This was not acceptable to Bhutto, Yahya Khan and the military establishment in West Pakistan. They disregarded the verdict and the mandate delivered by the people. Sheikh Rahman decided to boycott the session of the National Assembly scheduled for 3 March 1971. Yahya Khan postponed the inauguration of the assembly session. His move precipitated a showdown and confrontation between East and West Pakistan and, as a result, Sheikh Rahman launched a civil disobedience movement in East Pakistan. It was an overwhelming success, as the people of East Pakistan embraced it wholeheartedly and gave it their full support.

The hardliners of West Pakistan decided to teach the East Pakistanis a lesson. They replaced the governor of East Pakistan. A known hardliner and a hawk, Lt Gen. Tikka Khan was appointed the new governor of East Pakistan. As soon as he arrived in Dacca, he began the cruel and violent suppression of the people of East Pakistan. His cruel methods were to earn him the sobriquet 'Butcher of East Pakistan'. On the night of 25 March 1971, soldiers opened fire in Dacca with automatic weapons on unarmed civilians and spread terror among the public. There were widespread random killings of unarmed and innocent men and women. Universities, colleges and academic institutions were particularly targeted and attacked viciously, as they were the hotbeds of political activity and the seat of the resistance. The Pakistani army was given a free rein and it resorted to mass killings, arson and rape. The people of East Pakistan began to resist the repression, and the situation soon escalated into a civil war. Sheikh Rahman was arrested by the Pakistani military.

A wave of anger swept among the proud Bengalis of East Pakistan. In April 1971, the people of East Pakistan and the Awami League gave East Pakistan a new name, Bangladesh. They came together to constitute the Government of Bangladesh and declared Sheikh Mujibur Rahman as the president. West Pakistan persisted with its barbaric attacks on the Bengali population, and large-scale loot, arson and rape by the Pakistani army became routine.

The Exodus

Unable to bear the brutal oppression unleashed on them, the East Pakistanis began to cross the international border with India to seek safety and refuge from the daily savagery and brutality of the Pakistan Army. By August 1971, more than six million people had crossed over into India and sought refuge.[1] The burden of looking after such a huge number of refugees began to tell on the Indian resources. India had to set up hundreds of camps

---

[1]Nanda, S.M., *The Man Who Bombed Karachi: A Memoir*, HarperCollins Publishers India, 2004, p. 183.

to provide shelter, food, clothing, medical assistance and other essential necessities to the refugees, whose number swelled to eight million. This began to severely stress the meagre resources of India, and also created serious problems of crowding, and scarcity of food and essentials for the residents of the Indian states.

India tried to bring the problem to the notice of the leaders of the US and other major Western countries to help resolve the heavy influx of refugees into India. In October 1971, the then PM Indira Gandhi personally visited the world capitals and held discussions with the senior leadership of the Western countries. She visited the US, the UK and some other European countries to explain India's case, but the world paid little attention to India's pleadings, and showed no urgency or concern. On the contrary, the Western powers and China seemed to be biased and in favour of Pakistan, and regarded the whole issue as the internal affair of Pakistan.

India made every effort to resolve the problem, but there appeared to be no solution in sight. Therefore, India decided to take matters into its own hands by creating suitable conditions in East Pakistan for the refugees to return to their own country. This meant waging a war with Pakistan and neutralizing the Pakistani army in East Pakistan. India decided that if that was the only solution to the problem, so be it.

In April 1971, PM Indira Gandhi held a meeting with the Chief of Army Staff, Gen. S.H.F.J. (popularly known as Sam) Manekshaw. She informed the General that the refugee situation had become intolerable and India had no option except to consider the military option. The General recommended that it would be advisable to wait till monsoons were over. It was decided to go ahead with the military option sometime in November 1971. The PM left it to the General to work out the details with the Indian Navy, the Indian Army and the IAF for consolidated action.

Gen. Sam Manekshaw was a soldier decorated with the Military Cross, a gallantry award for distinguished services in action. He was widely known as Sam Bahadur. In recognition of his services in the 1971 war, Gen. Manekshaw was promoted to the rank of field marshal on 1 January 1973, becoming the first Indian Army officer to hold this rank.

Thus, the stage was set for a war with Pakistan. The details of this war from the Indian naval aviation's point of view are narrated in the chapters that follow.

≈

6

The *Vikrant* in 1970–71

In all the previous wars that India had fought since Independence in 1947, it was always the Indian Army and IAF that did the heavy lifting during the conflict and the fighting. The Indian Navy did not deploy in an offensive role during the Sino-Indian war in 1962 or in the 1965 war against Pakistan. During the 1965 Indo-Pak War, INS *Vikrant* was in dry docks, undergoing refit and repairs in the Naval Dockyard at Bombay. This had dented the navy's reputation and lowered the expectations of the national defence planners. The navy's role in India's conflicts and wars was considered of little consequence.

The navy was extremely uncomfortable with such an impression among the sister services, and the nation at large. The top brass of the Indian Navy felt strongly that such a wrong impression would be damaging for them even more if it was allowed to persist and steps were not taken to correct it. They felt they must take remedial measures soon, to redeem the navy's reputation as one of the major armed forces of the country.

Signs of Age

From around 1968, there was no escaping the fact that the *Vikrant* and the Sea Hawks were showing signs of wear and tear due to age. The *Vikrant* was now about 25 years old and had begun to show signs of deterioration in her systems. Despite the best efforts devoted to the ship, the Indian Navy's marine engineers were experiencing maintenance and operational problems with the *Vikrant*'s steam catapult, arrester gear and boilers—the three most important parts of her systems that dealt with her power to move and her ability to operate her aircraft, her main armament.

In mid-1970, during the *Vikrant*'s deployment in the Bay of Bengal, engineers had detected cracks in the endcaps of the water drum of one of the four main boilers. This was serious and jeopardized the safety of the boiler and the ship, as the boiler could potentially explode, causing severe damage. The experts advised against using this boiler when sailing and recommended replacement of the defective steam drum of the boiler. Replacing the drum of the *Vikrant*'s boiler was major work, and estimates indicated she would be out of operation for the next three to four years, as the new drum was not available off the shelf and had a lead time for supply of about three years by the manufacturers.

Thus, in 1970, as the war clouds began to gather on the horizon for India and Pakistan, the *Vikrant* once again found herself on the wrong side. She was yet again helplessly tied alongside a jetty in the Naval Dockyard, Bombay, with little prospect of putting to sea and taking part in the action. It meant that the frontline squadrons, INAS 300 of the Sea Hawk jet fighters and INAS 310 operating the anti-submarine Alizé aircraft, would not be embarking on the aircraft carrier for the next three years or so.

With the prospect of the *Vikrant* remaining out of operation for three to four years, the ship and the squadrons began to post out their pilots, engineers and other personnel. It was a disappointing and embarrassing situation for the Indian Navy because a technical snag precluded the biggest aircraft carrier from taking part in the impending war with Pakistan.

Strategic Decisions

In June 1970, the *Vikrant* was still docked at the Naval Dockyard, Bombay. Naval headquarters issued orders not to use the defective boiler until further notice, effectively grounding the ship.

However, this wasn't entirely safe, neither for the *Vikrant* nor the fate of India if war was to break out. As part of the Western fleet, INS *Vikrant* was based in Bombay. Karachi, the main sea port and the home of the warships of the Pakistan Navy, was located at the northern end of the Arabian Sea. This was a geographical constraint for Pakistan. The ships and submarines of the Pakistan Navy could sail out of Karachi and go to open waters of the Indian Ocean in the southward direction only. This was the only sea route for the Pakistani ships to go from West Pakistan to the Bay of Bengal and from there to East Pakistan, sailing around the southern tip of the Indian mainland.

The distance from Karachi to Chittagong by sea was 2,900 nautical miles (5,370 km) and, at a speed of 10 knots, it would take a ship 12 days at sea to complete the journey. When sailing out from Karachi, the Pakistani warships had to sail in southerly direction to go to the Indian Ocean or to East Pakistan. All this time, Indian coastline of Gujarat and Maharashtra was on their left. This was the area of operation of the Indian Navy's warships and submarines of the Western Naval Command based in Bombay. In 1970–71, there was an expert assessment that some Pakistani submarines had an edge over the submarines of the Indian Navy, especially the three Daphné-class submarines the Pakistan Navy had acquired. Therefore, there was a clear perception of a submarine threat from the Pakistan submarines to the Indian naval ships operating in the Arabian Sea.

Bombay was also the home port of INS *Vikrant* and she, too, was under threat. The *Vikrant* was the flagship of the Indian Navy. The air squadrons of the ship could play a decisive role in the outcome of any war with Pakistan. The *Vikrant* was, however, vulnerable to a Pakistani submarine attack when operating in the Arabian Sea. It was a large ship and, therefore, a big target for an enemy submarine lurking below waters, or for a desperate attack by an enemy fighter aircraft, or even a determined group of terrorists. The loss of the ship of the size and importance of the *Vikrant* could have been the most serious blow not only to the Indian Navy but also to India. In such an event, there would be little doubt in the minds of the international observers as to who won and who lost the war. In the late 1970s, the Indian naval top brass recommended that the *Vikrant* be moved out of harm's way from Bombay to the Bay of Bengal under the Eastern Naval Command situated at Visakhapatnam.

On 26 February 1971, the ship was moved from Ballard Pier Extension to the anchorage. The main objective behind this move was to light up the other three boilers at reduced pressure, and workup the main and flight deck machinery that had been lying idle for almost seven months. On 1 March, the boilers were ignited, and basin trials up to 40 revolutions per minute (RPM) were conducted. Catapult trials were conducted on the same day. The ship carried out sea trials between 18 March and 27 April 1971. The Indian Navy decided to limit the boilers to a steam pressure of 400 pounds per sq. inch. This reduced the ship's speed to 14 knots (26 km/hr) from the designed speed of 25 knots (46 km/hr). Accordingly, in April 1971, the naval headquarters issued instructions to the Naval Dockyard, Bombay, to make the *Vikrant* seaworthy on priority.

The *Vikrant* completed her sea trials in Bombay by June-end in 1971 and was declared seaworthy. After the extensive repairs at the Naval Dockyard, the ship, however, had a crippling limitation: the maximum speed of 14 knots (26km/hr) prohibited the take-offs and landings by the fixed-wing aircraft from the *Vikrant's* deck. This restriction severely affected the capability of the ship to launch and recover aircraft, because flying operations were heavily dependent upon the speed of the natural wind available on the flight deck of the ship.

What was important now was that the *Vikrant* could sail under her own power. Naval headquarters ordered to send her from the Western Naval Command, Bombay, to the Eastern Naval Command, Visakhapatnam, in the Bay of Bengal. This served two objectives. First, it removed the *Vikrant* from the Arabian Sea, where she could have been a target for the Pakistan submarines and even shore-based aircraft. The second was that the *Vikrant*, her jet fighters and anti-submarine aircraft could potentially be used in the Bay of Bengal to cut off East Pakistan from any help from West Pakistan or anyone else. However, there was a serious flaw in this vision. The *Vikrant's* defective boiler prevented her from launching and recovering Alizés and Sea Hawks. This would again result in the *Vikrant* sitting out a potential war with Pakistan. But Admiral S.M. Nanda, the CNS at the time, would have none of it.

A Reputation at Stake

Admiral Nanda was the CNS from February 1970 to February 1973. He was at the helm of the Indian Navy in the period leading to and during the days of the Indo-Pak War. He was of the firm belief that Indian Navy had to demonstrate to the nation the potential of the naval power at sea by obtaining positive results during the next conflict or war.

Commenting on the Indian Navy's lack of participation in national wars in 1965 and earlier, Admiral S.M. Nanda writes in *The Man Who Bombed Karachi: A Memoir*:

> There were other incidents that singled out the Navy as being inconsequential in a national war. All these factors

strengthened my resolve to lift the service out of the doctrinal straitjacket in which it had been confined. I was determined, if given a chance, to restore the Navy to its rightful place among the major actors on India's national security scene.[1]

In an article published in the tabloid *Blitz* of Bombay (15 March 1969), Admiral Nanda had written: 'And if war comes again, I assure you that we shall carry it right into the enemy's biggest ports like Karachi. I know the harbour quite well for I started my career working there. And you have my word that given the opportunity, the Indian Navy will make the world's biggest bonfire of it.'[2]

Moreover, as war with Pakistan was becoming a distinct possibility, the Indian Navy began to move its ships to preferred locations in Indian waters. The serviceability of the *Vikrant* was a serious concern and Capt. G.M. Hiranandani, fleet operations officer, quotes Admiral Nanda as having said, '...during the 1965 war, *Vikrant* was sitting in Bombay harbour and did not go out to sea. If the same thing happened in 1971, *Vikrant* would be called a white elephant and naval aviation would be written off. *Vikrant* has to be seen being operational even if we don't fly any aircraft.'[3] Admiral Nanda and Capt. Hiranandani were determined to make *Vikrant* operational, especially since both of them believed in the significance of the *Vikrant* in affecting the outcome of a war with Pakistan. Admiral Nanda wrote:

One might think that the final deployment of *one* ship may make but little difference to the final outcome of a war, but the history of the maritime encounters is replete with instances wherein the performance (either successful or

[1]Nanda, S.M., *The Man Who Bombed Karachi: A Memoir*, HarperCollins Publishers India, 2004, p. 178.
[2]Ibid. 174.
[3]Hiranandani, G.M., *Transition to Triumph: History of the Indian Navy, 1965-1975*, Spantech & Lancer, 2000.

unsuccessful) of a single capital ship has affected the course of many wars. In the subcontinental arena, the *Vikrant* was certainly a giant vessel. Although weighing only 20,000 tons, the air squadrons of the ship did play a decisive role in the outcome of the 1971 war.[4]

Admiral Hiranandani strikes a similar note in his book *Transition to Triumph—Indian Navy 1965-75,* when he states:

> In retrospect, *Vikrant's* contribution to naval operations was beyond anyone's expectations. *Vikrant* stretched everything and everybody to the limit to launch and recover aircraft. In addition to the achievements of the air strikes, *Vikrant's* assistance in contraband control was invaluable. Without *Vikrant*, the limited number of ships that constituted the Eastern Fleet could not have coped with the task.[5]

Preparing the *Vikrant* for War

With the boiler becoming non-functional, the *Vikrant* could not operate her most potent weapons, the jet fighter Sea Hawks and the anti-submarine Alizés. She could not launch them and she could not recover them, as both operations required the ship to attain a minimum speed, which would be impossible with one boiler down. As a war machine, she was useless without the ability to sail and operate her air squadrons.

Admiral Nanda decided that the Indian Navy had to adopt an offensive and aggressive strategy against hostile Pakistan. He began to hold meetings with the top brass of the navy at naval

---

[4]Nanda, S.M., *The Man Who Bombed Karachi: A Memoir,* HarperCollins Publishers India, 2004. p. 198.
[5]Hiranandani, G.M., *Transition to Triumph: History of the Indian Navy, 1965-1975,* Spantech & Lancer, 2000.

headquarters and in the Eastern and Western Commands to build consensus to his way of thinking. India's only aircraft carrier INS *Vikrant* was acquired in 1961, but neither the *Vikrant* nor its fighter squadrons of Sea Hawks and Alizés had ever been used in an offensive role except briefly during the liberation of Goa.

Admiral Nanda and Vice Admiral N. Krishnan, the commander-in-chief of Eastern Naval Command at Visakhapatnam, were determined to find ways and means to make the *Vikrant* operational for flying operations even with one of her boilers defective. Recalling the *Vikrant*'s deployment in the Bay of Bengal in 1971, Admiral Nanda wrote about how the speed restriction was proving to be a difficulty in the normal operation of aircraft from on board the ship. The aircraft were operating from the Madras airport. 'To maintain his pilots in flying trim, Captain Parkash [the commanding officer of INS *Vikrant*] ordered the Alizés to only practice "rollers"[6] whenever the fresh afternoon breeze gave him extra knots on deck.'

Both the admirals embarked on board INS *Vikrant* in August 1971. They held detailed discussions with Capt. Swaraj Parkash, Cdr Benoy Roy Chowdhury, the engineer officer of the ship, and other key officers. The Sea Hawk Squadron INAS 300 was waiting ashore at Meenambakam, Madras, with six Sea Hawks but could not embark because the *Vikrant* had been restrained by the naval headquarters from launching and arresting fixed-wing aircraft.

The Naval Dockyard, Bombay, had put a steel strop or band on the defective boiler to strengthen the water drum and contain the spread of the cracks when under steam pressure. The ship's engineers were not convinced of the safety of operating the defective boiler due to risk of its explosion.

---

[6]Rollers refer to the act of aircraft slowing down enough for its wheels to roll along the deck surface and getting airborne again without actually landing or halting on deck.

A solution popped up during these discussions. In his book, Admiral Nanda wrote:

> Whilst all the discussions centred around the methods to contain the crack, an idea suddenly occurred to me. I asked, 'Where does the oil to the boilers come from?' I was shown the control valve near the upper deck. Immediately, I saw a way of overcoming the misgiving of the crew and suggested that the boiler room be left unmanned while using the aircraft catapults. One man could be positioned at the oil flow control valve ready to cut off supply to the boiler in case of an emergency.
>
> The idea was discussed and debated at length. I decided to take that calculated risk and be on hand to see them implement my decision. The Alizés and Sea Hawks were hooked and catapulted in my presence. This manoeuvre was followed by permission from the naval headquarters to embark both the Alizé and Sea Hawk squadrons.[7]

This solution allowed a relatively safe operation of the boiler. Admiral Nanda approved this solution and gave the go-ahead to Capt. Parkash. The fourth boiler was fired and steam was raised. The ship's boilers were now able to raise enough pressure for the ship's steam catapult to launch the fixed-wing aircraft.

The ship could now gain enough speed and generate sufficient wind on flight deck to call in an Alizé aircraft stationed at Meenambakkam airport, to fly out to do rollers on the ship's flight deck to get a sense and a feel from the aircrew of the conditions on the flight deck when coming in to attempt a landing. This trial was successful. The Alizé was then asked to carry out an arrestor hook landing on the carrier. This, too, was successful and the Alizé landed on the ship. The same Alizé was

---

[7]Nanda, S.M., *The Man Who Bombed Karachi: A Memoir*, HarperCollins Publishers India, 2004, p. 202.

then launched from the ship's catapult and this launch, too, was satisfactory. Following this exercise, all Alizés of the INAS 310 were embarked on the carrier.

A similar exercise was undertaken for the Sea Hawks. First, one Sea Hawk was called in from Meenambakkam to do rollers on flight deck. After successful rollers, the pilot was asked to land on the ship, which was done successfully. The same Sea Hawk was launched from the ship by catapult the next morning. The Sea Hawk squadron was then cleared to land on the ship. The aircraft carrier was now operational with both of her squadrons embarked on board and ready for normal flying operations from the carrier. The *Vikrant* was operational, much to everyone's relief, although she was somewhat short of her designed propulsion power and speed.

WORDS OF THE SQUADRON LEADER

Rear Admiral S.K. Gupta was the commanding officer of the Sea Hawk squadron INAS 300 during this time at INS Hansa, Dabolim, Goa. He recalls the state of the squadron in the late 1970s and the fast pace of the events of this period from the aviation perspective.

It soon became obvious that the disembarked period would be prolonged indefinitely while waiting for the water drum from the UK. The 300 Squadron then witnessed the appointments of freshly-inducted naval pilots who had recently earned their 'Wings' from the IAF flying academies, thus changing the role of the squadron from an operational one to one of training. There was a discerning change in the priorities now given to the erstwhile frontline squadron. The embarkation days seemed definitely over for the Sea Hawks.

The non-availability of the mother ship *Vikrant* had an adverse effect on the squadron. INAS 300 lost its prominence as a frontline operational fighter squadron, and instead took on a training role for newly-joined inexperienced pilots, to prepare them for embarked flying on the carrier.

There was, however, another setback, as aircraft spares had begun to run out. Major spares for the engine, such as the exhaust units and hot-ends, could only be manufactured in the UK against special and urgent orders, with long lead times and at exorbitant cost. The allocation of valuable foreign exchange depended on priorities, and the squadron now had none! In any case, until the *Vikrant*'s defective boiler became operational, there would be no embarkation. The availability of sufficient Sea Hawks came down. The next change was that the pilots with sufficient experience of deck landings were transferred out on staff or sea appointments, and were replaced by the relatively inexperienced pilots who had no experience in operating from the aircraft carrier.

This was the situation in the squadron in late June 1971, after the *Vikrant* sailed out to the Bay of Bengal to keep her out of harm's way. The Sea Hawk squadron was instructed to proceed to Madras to exercise with the carrier. The squadron was able to muster only four aircraft, which were ferry flown, with two more to join later, when available. Exercising with the *Vikrant* in the next three weeks gave confidence to both the ship and the pilots. On 17 August 1971, two pilots made arrested landings, which were then followed by catapult launches.[8] In the next six weeks, by September-end, there were five Sea Hawks on board.

Further, both the air technical officers were transferred out without replacement. This coincided with the period when demand was placed to detach six Sea Hawks to Madras. It was not until an experienced, mature, technically sound and energetic AEO, Lt Gurnam Singh, joined the squadron in Madras, accompanied by an inexperienced ALO, though very conscientious and quick to learn, Lt R. Shahdadpuri. There was almost an immediate improvement in the serviceability of the six aircraft positioned in Madras. By early October, aircraft spares began arriving for the Sea Hawks. Additional aircraft were allotted, so that by

---

[8]The length of INS *Vikrant* was 210 m. A jet fighter aircraft cannot take off or land in such a small distance. The method employed for an aircraft to fly from *Vikrant* was called 'launching'. A steam-operated machinery and device called 'catapult' assists the aircraft to become airborne. Similarly, an aircraft cannot land and come to a stop in such a short distance. Again, ship deploys a device, using which it catches the aircraft by its tail hook and helps it to land on board. This is called arrested landing.

October-end, there were 18 aircraft on board with 15 pilots. It was then a matter of a couple of weeks for the ship and her air squadrons to get operational. In 24 flying days, the mother ship and her squadrons were battle ready. When the Eastern Fleet came into being on the 3 November, the mother ship and her squadrons were fully operational and raring to go! By now the intentions of the CNS, the Eastern Naval Command and the Captain of the *Vikrant* became clear: to embark the two squadrons to play a proactive and an aggressive role in the war!

The Indian Navy had bought a total of 74 Sea Hawks—60 second-hand and 14 new. By mid-1971, 40 had been lost due to accidents and only 34 remained. One more was heavily damaged on 30 October 1971 just before the war. Thus, only 33 were available, out of which 18 went to war. The Indian Navy has the distinction of purchasing the used, second-hand reconditioned Sea Hawks, maintaining them in frontline service for embarked flying, and going to war in 1971 with 18 of these old flying machines, in intense and sustained carrier-borne operations. It is to the credit of the squadron that it maintained high serviceability of these aircraft in their operational role during the critical three to four months from September to December 1971, achieving 100 per cent availability on some days, when all 18 were serviceable for operations.

7

War Begins:
The Western Front

In a war situation, such as the one that was developing between India and Pakistan, it is natural for an adversary to gauge and assess the relative strengths, weaknesses and anticipated moves of the opponent. The adversaries tend to guard their respective strengths and the strategy with which they would deploy their forces. The armed forces call such exercises war games. Each tries to gain maximum advantage for himself and inflict maximum damage to the adversary. To facilitate such assessment, nations collect intelligence about the armed forces and the assets of other countries, especially of their adversaries.

The 1971 Indo-Pak War was no different, and the Indian Navy organized and played the war games regularly to understand what Pakistan was likely to do. There are memoirs of generals, admirals and air-marshals of the war in which they reveal what they did or did not do and what was the outcome.

Those who were on the winning side write about the strategy and deployment of their forces. Those who lost also write to explain and justify the way they conducted the battles, operations and wars, and sometimes inform readers why they lost.

There are enough books written about the 1971 war, each from the author's unique point of view. They form an open pool of information for researchers. It is now known that, departing from the practices of the earlier years, in the 1971 war, the Indian Navy brass had decided to go on high offensive as soon as the war was declared, and hit first and hit hard in both the eastern and the western theatres. The Indian Navy also deployed its forces, adopting unconventional strategies which Pakistan could not understand or anticipate. The Indian Navy was able to foretell the way Pakistan Navy would deploy its assets during war, and accordingly plan measures to neutralize Pakistan Navy before it could put its planned strategy in motion.

Recalling such exercises at the command and the headquarters level as the war approached, Admiral Nanda wrote:

> Having established through simulation that Pakistan Navy could obviously not be everywhere, the operations staff began to gain confidence in the idea of storming citadel Karachi. A series of games played using the tactical simulator made it clear that our missile boats could be used during the dark hours with success, as the Pakistan Air Force had no night strike capability at sea.[1]

The Indian Navy put this strategy in operation. It decided that on declaration of war, Karachi should be attacked immediately. The attack must be ferocious to put Pakistan Navy warships, naval installations in the port, fuel farms, infrastructure and warship repair facilities in the Karachi harbour out of operation. A surprise missile attack by newly acquired missile boats was planned and executed brilliantly. The Indian Navy struck Karachi twice, sinking the Pakistan fleet's major warships and seriously damaging other assets. The strategy was brilliant and worked to near perfection,

---

[1]Nanda, S.M., *The Man Who Bombed Karachi: A Memoir*, HarperCollins Publishers India, 2004, p. 192.

with no loss suffered by the Indian Navy. After the missile attack, the Pakistan Navy warships were bottled up in the Karachi harbour or dispersed at sea to escape attack by the Indian Navy. The Pakistan Navy did not take part in the war. The Indian Navy implemented a complete blockade of the Karachi harbour from the Arabian Sea. No ships could enter or leave Karachi without permission from the Indian Navy.

By carrying out successful blockades, devastation of ports and harbours, and closing down escape routes for the Pakistan forces in the east, the navy's Eastern Fleet facilitated the Indian ground operations. Lt Gen. J.S. Aurora, the general officer-in-chief of the Eastern Command, while addressing the personnel of the carrier after the operations, said that it had 'reduced the task of the Army threefold in the eastern sector'.[2]

In 1970–71, Pakistan, too, was aware that its navy did not measure up to the Indian counterpart for an out-and-out naval conflict. It was neither a match for a test of strength and battle at sea with the Indian Navy nor was it able to defend against the Indian Navy's attack on Pakistan's naval assets and infrastructure concentrated in Karachi.

---

[2]Prasad, S.N., and U.P. Thapliyal (eds), *The India-Pakistan War of 1971: A History*, Natraj Publishers, 2019, p. 396.

Table 1
Relative Strength of India and Pakistan Navies

In the West[3]		
Ship	**Indian Navy**	**Pakistan Navy**
Submarine	2	3
Cruisers	1	1
Destroyers/frigates	15	5
Auxiliaries and smaller vessels	28	34
Total	46	43
In the East[4]		
Ship	**Indian Navy**	**Pakistan Navy**
Submarines	1	1
Aircraft carriers	1	-
Destroyers/frigates	5	-
Landing ships/crafts	3	2
Tankers	1	-
Smaller vessels	4	51

While the Indian Navy deployed its ships to control and dominate the Bay of Bengal as per its strategic plans, the Pakistan Naval Fleet in the east comprised ships that could operate mostly in the harbours and inland waterways.

---

[3]Ibid. 246.
[4]Ibid. 375.

Operation Trident

Pakistan has only one large sea port, Karachi, which is situated in the north of the Arabian Sea. In 1971, the headquarters of Pakistan Navy and nearly all its warships were based in Karachi. This city was, and remains, the hub of Pakistan's international sea commerce and trade. Pakistan's economy depends heavily on the maritime trade of Karachi. Indian naval planners came to the conclusion that destruction of Karachi by a naval attack, followed by its blockade from the seaside, would be disastrous for Pakistan's defensive and offensive capabilities as well as its economy. Such an operation would choke Pakistan, move it to economic ruin and demoralize it. This would also neutralize the offensive capability of the Pakistan Navy against the Indian naval assets in the Arabian Sea and elsewhere because it would then be totally focussed on defending whatever would be left of Karachi after the Indian Navy's attack. It was a win-win strategy for India, because with the Pakistani naval warships bottled up in Karachi, India would not have to worry about an attack from Pakistan. This strategy and assessment proved to be correct. It determined the course of the 1971 war in Indian Navy's favour.

In November 1971, when tension between India and Pakistan was rising and Pakistan declared a national emergency on 23 November, the Indian Navy deployed three missile boats of Vidyut-class in the Okha area on the Gujarat coast. It was the closest the Indian warships could get to Karachi since hostilities had not been declared between the two nations at that point. These missile boats were deployed at Okha for sea surveillance of the traffic and movements of the Pakistani warships, the merchant ships and aircraft. Operating the missile boats from Okha helped the commanding officers and their men in getting familiarized with the sea, weather, wind conditions, visibility at sea, shipping traffic and other operational parameters. This also tested and proved the missile boats operating facilities established at Okha.

On 3 December, Pakistani aircraft attacked Indian airfields along the border in the western sector, and war was declared. As strategized by Admiral Nanda, the Indian Navy had made plans to take the offensive approach and mount a massive naval attack on Karachi and the Pakistani fleet in the harbour as soon as the war began. A Karachi Strike Group had been formed under Cdr Babru Bhan Yadav, who was commanding the Missile Boat Squadron. The Group consisted of three Vidyut-class missile boats—INS *Nipat*, INS *Nirghat* and INS *Veer*. The missile boats of the Karachi Strike Group were positioned at Okha. Each of the three boats was armed with four Styx missiles with a range of 74 km. Two anti-submarine corvettes, INS *Kiltan* and INS *Katchall*, and a fleet tanker INS *Poshak*, accompanied the missile boats and provided support to them during and after the attacking operations. Admiral Nanda took a bold decision to use the just-arrived missile boats from the Union of Soviet Socialist Republics (USSR) to carry out a massive missile attack on Karachi, within a day of the declaration of war between India and Pakistan. The missile boats were designed and acquired for the coastal defence of India and the Indian harbours but Admiral Nanda decided to use them to attack Karachi, 200 km by sea, from the nearest Indian sea port of Okha. Missile boats could not sail that far, as they were not designed for such an extended operation at high seas. It was decided that the larger warships would tow the missile boats to the enemy water till Karachi was within the range of their missiles. It was an out of the box bold decision and a brilliant one.

On 4 December, the Karachi Strike Group reached 460 km south of the coast of Karachi. It had been calculated that at this distance, the group would be outside the range of the Pakistan Air Force (PAF). It was known to the Indian naval planners that the PAF did not possess night bombing capabilities. The strike group, therefore, had planned to attack Karachi at night, between dusk and dawn. At 10.30 p.m., the Indian task group took up their position at the sea, south of Karachi. When approaching the harbour, at about 130 km from it, the Karachi Strike Group detected Pakistani warships to the northwest and the northeast.

INS *Nirghat* moved in the northwest direction and fired its first missile at PNS *Khaibar*, a battle-class destroyer. The missile found its target and hit the warship on its right side, causing heavy damage and explosion in the *Khaibar*'s boiler room. The ship lost its main engines and its propulsion power. It was filled with fire and smoke. The sea had begun to enter the ship, but it stayed afloat and became a stationary target. The *Nirghat* fired its second missile, hitting the *Khaibar* and sinking the ship.

At 11.00 p.m., the *Nipat* detected two targets in the northwest direction and fired two missiles, one each at cargo vessel MV *Venus Challenger* and its escort, PNS *Shah Jahan*, a destroyer. The *Venus Challenger* was a merchant ship, carrying ammunition for the Pakistani forces. With the missile scoring a direct hit, the ship exploded and sank 43 km south of Karachi. The other missile hit the destroyer *Shah Jahan*, causing heavy damage. INS *Veer* targeted a minesweeper *Muhafiz* and scored a hit. It, too, sank immediately.

INS *Nipat* continued towards Karachi. Positioning itself 26 km south of Karachi harbour, it targeted the Keamari Oil Tank fuel farms. Two missiles were launched, one misfired, but the other hit the oil tanks, starting huge fires. The conflagration of the oil fires destroyed many of the fuel storage tanks. It led to a serious fuel shortage for the warships of Pakistan and adversely affected the subsequent operation of the Pakistani fleet. The attack and the operation completed, the Karachi Strike Group withdrew from the attack zone and headed south. It returned safely to Indian waters. The PAF retaliated by bombing Okha. The Indian Navy had anticipated such an attack and had taken it into account in the plans. After the attack, the Indian naval ships at Okha were moved to safer locations in the south.[5]

---

[5]Prasad, S.N., and U.P. Thapliyal (eds), *The India Pakistan War of 1971: A History*, Natraj Publishers, 2019, p. 254, 260.

The Pakistan Navy and its security forces were thrown into utter confusion. They were not able to determine who had attacked Karachi—the Indian Navy or the IAF. Were they attacked by bombs or by missiles? With such confusion prevailing, Pakistan attacked its own frigate *Zulfiquar*, mistaking it to be an Indian warship.

With no casualties on the Indian side, this operation is considered to be one of the most successful in modern naval history in the post-Second World War era. Pakistan lost warships and merchant ships carrying ammunition, and about 720 men, crippling the Pakistan Navy and its will for further participation in the war. To mark this victory, the Indian Navy annually celebrates Navy Day on 4 December.

This attack was planned and executed by Admiral S.M. Nanda; Vice Admiral Sourendra Nath Kohli, FOC-in-C, western naval command; and Rear Admiral Kuruvilla, the FOC, western fleet. After successful implementation of Operation Trident, other officers involved were honoured with gallantry awards. Capt. (later vice admiral) G.M. Hiranandani, the fleet operations officer, was awarded Nao Sena Medal for planning the operation. The Karachi Strike Group commander, Babru Bhan Yadav, was conferred with MVC—he had planned the attack and led the task force. Cdr S.P. Gopal Rao, the commanding officer of INS *Kiltan*, which towed the missile boats to Karachi, was awarded the MVC. Vir Chakras were awarded to Lt Cdr Nariman Kavina, Lt Cdr Inderjit Sharma and Lt Cdr Om Prakash Mehta, the commanding officers of INS *Nipat*, INS *Nirghat* and INS *Veer*, respectively. Master Chief M.N. Sangal of INS *Nirghat* was awarded the Vir Chakra (VrC) for his role in the attack.

Operation Python

After Operation Trident, the Indian Navy found that the oil storage facilities in Karachi were still operational. The reason was that out of the two missiles fired at the facilities, only one had hit the target. Operation Python was launched three days later to put the Karachi harbour oil facilities out of operation.

On the night of 8/9 December, at 10.00 p.m. PKT (Pakistan Standard Time), a strike group of Indian naval warships approached Manora, a peninsula south of the Port of Karachi. The strike group consisted of missile boat INS *Vinash* and two frigates— INS *Talwar* and INS *Trishul*. The *Vinash* was equipped with four missiles. During their voyage to the operational area, the ships encountered a Pakistani patrol vessel and sunk it.

An hour later, around 11.00 p.m., the strike group detected a batch of Pakistani ships at a distance of 22 km. The *Vinash* immediately fired four of its missiles. The first of these hit the fuel tanks of the Keamari Oil Farm of Karachi harbour. The fuel tanks caught fire and there was a huge explosion. The second missile hit the Panamanian fuel tanker SS Gulf Star, sinking it. The third and fourth missiles hit the fleet tanker PNS *Dacca* and a British merchant ship *Harmattan*. The *Dacca* suffered heavy damage, but the *Harmattan* sank. Since the *Vinash* had fired all the four missiles, the group left the area immediately for the nearest Indian port. Remarkably, India suffered no loss of men or material. The commanding officer of INS *Vinash*, Lt Cdr Vijai Jerath, was awarded the VrC for this operation.

With Operation Trident and Operation Python, and the IAF attacks on Karachi's fuel and ammunition depots, more than half of the oil fuel capacity of Karachi had been destroyed and the Pakistani economy had been dealt a devastating blow. These attacks had destroyed the infrastructure of oil storage tanks, along with the fuel stored in them, ammunition depots and their ammunition and engineering facilities. Scarcity of fuel oil adversely affected the operations of the Pakistan Navy and the PAF.

The surprise element and the severity of these attacks demoralized the Pakistan Navy. The neutral merchant vessels started to avoid going to Karachi. If they had to, they would seek safe passage from the Indian authorities. The Indian Navy's actions had caused a virtual naval blockade of Karachi.

INS *KHUKRI*: A SURVIVOR REMEMBERS

In December 1971, Pritam Singh Moga, chief electrical artificer, was serving on board INS Khukri, *one of the anti-submarine frigate warships of the Indian Navy, as chief-in-charge of electronic equipment. He retired in 1976 and lives in Moga, Punjab, where he is associated with the Red Cross. He has narrated his experience on board this ship, when on 9 December 1971, the Pakistani submarine* Hangor *sank INS* Khukri *in the Arabian Sea.[6] Capt. Mahendra Nath Mulla, the commanding officer of INS* Khukri, *was on board the ship and went down with it. He was decorated posthumously with the MVC.*

On 2 December 1971, INS *Khukri* sailed from Bombay harbour at 9.00 a.m. We had an uneventful and normal sailing in the Arabian Sea. On 4 December, she was on operational duty in company of two other ships, INS *Kirpan* and INS *Kuthar*. Hostilities had just been declared between India and Pakistan.

On 5 December, INS *Kuthar*, INS *Kirpan* and INS *Khukri*—the three ships from the anti-submarine ship squadron of the Indian Navy—were sailing in the Arabian Sea off the Gujarat coast. While sailing, the main boiler of INS *Kuthar* developed a snag. She could not raise steam to generate power with her main engines. INS *Kirpan* was tasked to tow her back to Bombay harbour. INS *Khukri* was to escort the two ships.

The same day at noon, INS *Khukri* detected a submarine contact on her sonar. The commanding officer of INS *Khukri* gave the order to fire a mortar at the

[6]This account was shared with Commodore Gurnam Singh over two interviews.

submarine. The mortar was fired, exploding about three furlongs away from our ship. We heard the explosion of the mortar fired by us and then, after a short interval, we heard another explosion. The gunnery staff of INS *Khukri* was certain that the second explosion was not from the mortar fired by us. Soon after the second explosion, traces of oil appeared on the sea surface. It was a clear and bright day, so the oil patch could be distinctly seen on the sea surface.

The oil patch was a telltale sign that the submarine had been hit and damaged as well. Soon, INS *Khukri* lost contact with the submarine. Later, after the war, it was learnt that the engagement that day was with PNS *Hangor*. Though damaged from the mortar fired by INS *Khukri*, she was not mortally wounded. She was able to escape from the scene of the engagement. Despite being damaged, she remained seaworthy and continued on duty in her area of operation. She presumably sat on the seabed to prevent detection by INS *Khukri*. Submarines follow this tactic when trapped by surface warships with anti-submarine weapons capability. This was probably the reason why INS *Khukri* had lost contact with her.

INS *Khukri* continued to escort the convoy of the *Kirpan* towing the *Kuthar* to Bombay. The three ships arrived at Bombay the next day, on 6 December at about 8.00 a.m. The FOC-in-C (West) came on board INS *Khukri* to discuss about the incident with our commanding officer and staff. We had the audio recordings of the previous day's events and we played back the tapes for the admiral. He listened to the tapes attentively and appreciated the action taken by the commanding officer of INS *Khukri*, Capt. Mulla.

On the morning of 8 December 1971, INS *Kirpan* and INS *Khukri* sailed out of Bombay harbour in the northerly direction towards the sea, off Diu, Gujarat. INS *Kuthar* stayed back in Bombay for repairs to her boiler.

INS *Khukri* had two sonars. One was the ship's main sonar. It was also the ship's attack sonar. The second was the secondary sonar of the ship and it did not have the capability to attack. The primary sonar of INS *Khukri* had the submarine detection range of 3,000 yards, whereas the Daphné-class submarine, to which the PNS *Hangor* belonged, had a firing range of 6 nautical miles. INS *Khukri* was, therefore, outmatched in this technical aspect. Later on, I heard that after both had retired from their respective services, the then commanding officer of PNS *Hangor*, Capt. Tasmin Ahmed, met one of the survivors of INS *Khukri*, Lt Sharma, the then communication officer, and told him that it was PNS *Hangor* that was involved in the incident on 5 December with INS *Khukri*.

On 9 December, we were sailing in the Arabian Sea about 40 miles off Diu on the western coast of Gujarat. At about 8.45 p.m., the ship's company had finished their evening meals. They were relaxing in their respective messes, chatting among themselves or listening to their favourite music on their personal handsets, reading, playing card games, writing letters home or attending to their personal chores.

The broadcaster had just started reading the Hindi news when there was a loud explosion from the stern. The ship shuddered and shook. At that time, I was in the chief petty officers' mess located in the forward section of the ship. The explosion and the loud noise stunned everyone for a moment. The thought that something ominous had happened to the ship struck us. The gravity of the situation dawned upon all of us and we left the mess hurriedly. Everyone ran to their assigned action station in the ship following the shortest route.

After what appeared only a few moments, the ship received a second hit. It was also accompanied by a very loud explosion and the ship lost her electrical power instantaneously. The lights went out in the ship, and areas below decks and all machinery compartments and spaces were plunged into pitch darkness. A couple of minutes or so later, the *Khukri* was hit for the third time with as much ferocity. This was the crippling and fatal blow to the ship. The *Khukri* started to list to the starboard side.[7]

Three torpedoes had hit INS *Khukri*, all on her starboard side. It was night, it was dark and there was no light anywhere on the ship. No one knew who was where. All means of communication on the ship, personal or public, and all command and control had collapsed. Confusion prevailed. Seawater was entering the ship and she had started to list and her stern had begun to sink. Now each man on the ship was for himself as he struggled with the prospect of the sinking ship and the invading sea to somehow save himself. Everyone had to find a safe path to abandon the ship.

After the first hit to the ship, I had left my mess deck and had hurried towards the ship's Sonar Control Room. It was situated midship, just below the ship's bridge. I had not yet reached it when the second explosion occurred and the ship lost all electrical power. Since there were no lights and no power, there was nothing I could do even if I were to find my way to the Control Room. I was looking

---

[7]Starboard is the naval term for right side when looking to the front of the ship. The left side of the ship is called port side.

for an escape route when the ship was hit for the third time. There were shouts and sounds from all directions. I could neither see anyone in the dark nor recognize the voices, since they were more of terrified people and less of orderly and recognizable persons. Everyone was trying to climb and reach a higher part of the ship since they could perceive that the ship was listing and sinking. All those who happened to be on the upper decks either jumped overboard, or were thrown out into the sea when the ship's listing increased and they could not keep their balance and stay upright. The front of the ship lifted up. Those on the ship's deck lost their foothold and grip of the steel deck on which they were standing. Soon the sink of the ship accelerated and became more pronounced. The stern of the ship was askew to the right side and had gone underwater. The forward part of the ship was turning askew to the starboard side and had lifted up out of the sea.

I knew that there was a monkey rope ladder to climb to the ship's steering wheelhouse. It was situated just behind the bridge and it was not far from where I stood. I was familiar with it. I groped my way in the dark. I found the rope ladder I was looking for and I took it to climb in the dark to the ship's steering wheel house. The ship was now badly listed to the starboard side.

It was a topsy-turvy world in there. No matter how much I tried, I could not maintain my balance. I was thrown off my feet. I hit something and fell towards the deck of the ship, which was now nearly vertical. The port side of the ship was by now angled nearly above my head. The sea water was rushing in and it entered unhindered from the starboard side, which was by now below the sea level, into the sea.

I was hearing fearful and dreadful sounds. There were swooshing sounds of air escaping from the spaces, which the seawater was progressively claiming and occupying. There were also dreadful and creaking sounds from the ship's steel bulkheads and other heavy structures of her mainframe, which were straining and bending, or twisting out of shape, giving way under the forces of the heavy sea making way into the *Khukri*. Luckily for me, the wheelhouse's bulkhead steel door on the ship's port side was open. I was now in the wheelhouse, floating on sea water.

More and more seawater gushed into the wheelhouse and swirled menacingly around me. It was dark and I could see nothing. The dread of losing my life was beginning to rise in me. It was my intuitional sense of space and direction that now guided my actions. The seawater was pushing me in all directions. Suddenly, the same gushing, swirling seawater took charge of my body, pushed me, carried me and threw me out of the open bulkhead door on the port side, out of the ship and into the open sea. I have some recollection of sliding down the ship's side and then hitting the water. I went down, but I was able to come up to the surface. I was bewildered and disoriented but had a providential escape from a certain death.

The whole thing had happened unexpectedly and with such suddenness that it took me some time to regain my senses, get my bearings and understand the new reality. I was shaken to the core, but I told myself repeatedly to calm down and think rationally. My life depended on it. It was a great relief to find myself floating in the open sea. But I was still very close to the ship. I was not completely away from danger.

When I was leaving my mess, I had picked up my life jacket from my bunk. In the ship, everyone on board had been issued a personal life jacket. This is a standard operating procedure. I had grabbed it and put it on instinctively when I was rushing out of the mess. When I was cast away in the open sea, the first thing I did was to recheck my life jacket. It had been a reflex action. I was relieved to find that it was still on my body. I rechecked whether it was securely fastened and strapped to my body. It kept me afloat and provided me the needed buoyancy in the open sea.

Like all experienced sea-going mariners and sailors, I knew innately that one must swim away from a sinking ship as quickly as possible. When a ship sinks, the surrounding seawater rushes to fill the spaces and everything floating close by is sucked and pulled down to follow the sinking ship. Realizing I was still in danger, I began to swim away from the ship with all my might. I was moving further away from the stricken ship, albeit slowly. The ship, by now, had become near vertical in the water and appeared to stand on her behind. Her front had risen out of water and was pointing skywards. She still held on in this unnatural position as if she was pausing to make up her mind. She was sinking and going down but she was doing so gradually. She was still not plunging into the sea rapidly as one would have expected her to do. I, thus, had a few more precious moments to increase my distance from the ship.

After I felt I had moved to a safe distance, I turned to look in the direction of the ship. In the next few moments, the *Khukri* appeared to stand nearly upright and vertical in the water. In the darkness of the night in the open sea, the ship appeared like a huge dark grey shadow against the dark night.

My heart went out for my ship, which was now going down to her watery grave. The sight filled me with great sadness, which cannot be put into words. I felt something very dear, a part of my life, being wrenched and torn out of me. Tears welled in my eyes and I began to sob uncontrollably. All I could do was lift up my right hand and give INS *Khukri*, my darling ship, a final awkward salute for the last time.

There has never been a sadder and more sombre moment in my life, ever. At that moment, I realized the sanctity and the sacredness of the bond that exists between a ship and those who sail in her. The separation was gut-wrenching, terrible and excruciatingly painful.

By now her stern was under water and her front was standing up vertically pointing skywards. INS *Khukri* was now just a surreal and dark shadow. With every passing moment, this shadow became smaller and smaller, reducing and diminishing right in front of my eyes. INS *Khukri* appeared to hesitate for a moment or two, and then she gradually plunged and sank, disappearing into the sea. There was nothing left of INS *Khukri*, the warship that had stood there just an hour ago, sailing in the waters of the Arabian Sea with no foreboding of the terrible events that were to unfold within the next hour. The sea had claimed her.

I desperately tried to compose myself. I was utterly lonely in the vast open sea, but I was alive. There was no more time to lose. It was dark. I could now hear in the distance some shouts and cries for help from my shipmates who, like me, were in the sea. I could only hear but not see them. I did not know how many made it out of the ship alive and how many went down with her.

The seawater in December off the coast of Gujarat was cold. There was a swell in the sea. The sea surface was black and as it rose and fell, I rose and fell with it. The waves were not gentle. They were drenching my head and face again and again. I was floating, and I bobbed up and down, rising and falling with the crest and fall of each wave. I heard some muffled sounds. They appeared to be coming from a distance. I could make out they were sounds of the depth charges exploding in the sea. I surmised they must have been fired by our sister ship INS *Kirpan* to scare away the submarine which might still be lurking underwater in the sea around us. I wondered if INS *Kirpan* would also fire her mortars against the submarine.

I continued to float in the sea. My eyes were smarting from the salt in the seawater, but I was also getting accustomed to the dark and could now see around, though somewhat dimly. After a while, I spotted the shape of a life raft, which was not very far from me. A life raft is a rubberized boat with a capacity of carrying 25 people. It has loops around it on its sides for 20 more people to hold on to it and float in the seawater, till help reaches and rescues them. Under normal circumstances, these are kept on board the ship, secured and lashed to the ship, on the upper deck. However, if sea water enters its release mechanism system, it gets activated. The life raft is automatically released from the ship and falls into the sea. These life rafts have a canopy of bright orange colour, which can be spotted from air or by the passing ships. I swam and reached close to this life raft, but it was not inflated yet.

I had to locate the rope that had to be pulled to inflate the raft. I located the rope—50-60 ft in length—and when I reached its end, I gave it a sharp jerk. This opened the valve of the compressed air cylinder on the life raft and the released compressed air inflated the life raft. The raft floated on water but it opened upside down; I made it upright. Then I shouted repeatedly at the top of my voice to let anybody in my vicinity know that I had a life raft. I heard some voices responding to my shouts, and soon I could make out from splashes in the water and their dim shapes that some people were swimming in my direction. They reached me one by one and I helped them climb the life raft.

I was still outside the life raft, but I held on to it. This way, I was able to help anyone approaching the raft. I saw a man swimming towards us. He had almost reached the raft but could not swim any more. He was starting to give up. A couple of seconds more and he would have drowned. I got hold of him and pulled him up. He was our Chief Telegraphist, C.T. John. Unfortunately, he passed away in 2014. There was yet another person whom I spotted close to me. I lunged forward and pulled him out, helping him climb the raft. He was Petty Officer Electrical Radio, Basra. I have not met him since.

Soon there were more than 25 people on board the life raft. I began to fear that the raft might get overloaded and capsize. I began to call those in the raft, requesting some of them to come out and float in the sea holding on to the life raft. No one paid any heed. I kept on shouting to attract the attention of anyone still in the water. There was no response. It seemed that all those who were floating within hearing distance had made it to the life raft.

I saw one more life raft floating near us. I got hold of it and managed to inflate it. Luckily, this one inflated correctly in one go. Half the people from the first raft were shifted to the second one. We lashed the two rafts together, so that they would float together and not drift away from each other.

When a life raft opens, a spot on its canopy lights up automatically. This is meant to be a light signal for the rescuers to see and spot the life raft, especially at night time. To ensure that our life rafts were not seen by the enemy submarine, which could have been lurking in the area, or by any other hostile enemy vessel, I broke the canopy lights of both the life rafts. Now, we were floating in the dark, and drifting at the mercy of the sea. I knew that we were about 40 nautical miles west of Diu on the coast of Gujarat.

We spent the night in the life rafts, in the open sea. Next day at the break of dawn, we saw a Super Constellation aircraft with Indian Navy markings flying in the sky above us. We waved to the aircraft and she dipped one wing indicating to us that she too had spotted us. At about 8.30 in the morning, we could see our sister ship INS *Kirpan* in the distance. It was approaching us. She had a rope net hanging on her port side. On approaching us, she slowed down and stopped alongside our life rafts. We climbed up by the net to the ship's deck, where we were received by the ship's staff.

It was a welcome relief from the harrowing ordeal of the previous night. When our feet touched the strong steel deck of the ship, it gave us the most reassuring feeling of being safe. After I had spent some time on INS *Kirpan*, I inquired them why the *Kirpan* did not fire mortars at the time the *Khukri* was hit. I learnt that their mortars had malfunctioned. The defect could not be rectified immediately. Since the submarine could be still lurking in the sea below, the *Kirpan* surmised that she could be the next target of the submarine. She took the wise decision and left the scene to go to a safe place. This also explained why she did not come and pick up the survivors from the sea after INS *Khukri* went down and sank. INS *Kirpan* brought us back to Bombay.

I served the Indian Navy for five more years and then retired. Today, there is a large-scale model of INS *Khukri* erected in Diu. It is placed on a hillock looking out westwards in the direction of the open Arabian Sea. There is also a museum in the memory of those of INS *Khukri* and my shipmates who lost their lives on that fateful night.

8

Confrontation at Sea: The Eastern Front

On the Eastern Front, in the Bay of Bengal, equal preparations were being made before war broke out in the west.

As part of preparations for the impending war with Pakistan, for better cohesion, administration, command and control, the Indian Navy created an Eastern Fleet in November 1971 with Rear Admiral S.H. Sarma as the first flag officer commanding eastern fleet (FOCEF). The Eastern Fleet consisted of INS *Vikrant*, the two frigates, INS *Brahmaputra* and INS *Beas*, the two Petya-class corvettes, INS *Kamorta* and INS *Kavaratti*, and one submarine INS Khanderi.

In the meantime, it was assessed that Pakistan would deploy its prized submarine, the PNS Ghazi, because of her range of operation away from her home port Karachi. The Indian Navy regarded the Ghazi a threat to the *Vikrant*. It was no secret that when *Vikrant* would start flying her aircraft, Pakistan would know her area of operation and target her.

INAS 300 Officers Recall

Commodore Gurnam Singh

Commodore Gurnam Singh was a lieutenant in 1971 and also the AEO of the Sea Hawk Squadron INAS 300. In 1970s, every young AEO dreamt of serving as the AEO of the elite squadron that was INAS 300. It had legendry reputation for its flying discipline and high standards. Gurnam Singh was no exception. He, thus, had an unmistakable glint in his eyes, prayer on his lips and a resolve to give his best to the squadron.

He joined the squadron at Meenambakam, Madras, in July 1971. He was the AEO of the squadron during the months leading to the war and fought in December 1971. He was responsible for all engineering aspects of the 18 Sea Hawks embarked on board the *Vikrant* and for ensuring their maximum availability. It is to his credit that the squadron repaired on board the battle damage from the Pakistani anti-aircraft guns that some of the Sea Hawks had suffered during their attack on the enemy positions in East Pakistan. Most of the damage to the aircraft and its systems was such that it could be repaired only at the naval repair yards ashore. Yet the squadron repaired the damage at the front line on the *Vikrant* itself, while the squadron continued waging war from the ship. During the 1971 war, 300 Squadron had five Sea Hawks, 13 ex-Germany and one German Sea Hawk IN 242, which met with an accident two months before the war. It was kept on board as a 'Christmas tree' to be robbed to meet the occasional demand of spares from the operational 18 Sea Hawks. The Sea Hawks in the squadron were:

Ex-Royal Navy (5): IN 155, IN 164, IN 167, IN 183 and IN 184

Ex-Germany (13): IN 230, IN 233, IN 234, IN 235, IN 236, IN 238, IN 239, IN 243, IN 247, IN 249, IN 250, IN 252 and IN 257

Accidented before the war (one Sea Hawk; used for spares): IN 242

Of these, three aircraft had already completed their life span of 15 years and most others had been refurbished before they were acquired. Two still had some life left, as they were brand new when purchased in 1961: IN 164 and IN 167. Being carrier-borne aircraft, these Sea Hawks had all been subjected to very high stress during their launch and recovery. The norms for the availability ratio of fighter aircraft were 60 per cent. Thus, for every 10 aircraft, six should have been serviceable at any given time, with the remaining four under maintenance and defect rectification. Since on account of their old age, all these aircraft were increasingly prone to defects, the availability ratio and the maintenance man-hours spent per flying hours went up significantly. Limited availability of spares also adversely affected the serviceability of the aircraft and their systems. Yet, it is to the credit of the 300 Squadron that its engineers maintained near 100 per cent serviceability at most times and repaired battle damage on board in the shortest possible time, and ensured that the damaged aircraft returned to the front line for flying.

After a month as the squadron AEO, Gurnam got the feel of the material state of the Sea Hawks in the squadron. He clearly saw his role as he got to know each Sea Hawk like the back of his hand, so as to know and understand the peculiarities of each aircraft and its systems. He kept a record of all the defects, the life of components and their time for replacement, including the engines and their hot-ends. He showed the charts he had prepared to the commanding officer (CO) of the squadron and the AEO of the *Vikrant*'s Air Engineering Department (AED) and projected the need to improve the material state of the aircraft. They agreed and gave him the go-ahead for his plans.

Gurnam adopted the policy of repair by replacement, rather than following the standard procedure of repairing the defective components and reinstalling them back on the aircraft. He passed instructions that all components that had completed 60 per cent of their lives were to be replaced with new components. Engine fuel pumps, hot-ends, engine starters—all were brought in for special scrutiny and replaced by new components. This meant that the squadron needed additional supply of new components. He prepared a list of all critical spares and gave it to the ship's senior AEO. A team was also formed to look into the aircraft ground equipment, like ladders, aircraft jacks, crocodile jacks, hydraulic trolleys, aircraft lashings and chocks. The electrical, radio and ordnance sections were also asked to undertake similar exercises. There were some defects like fuel leaks from the aircraft drop tanks, which used to occur when the Sea Hawks were on the catapult for launch, leading to the cancellation of the launch. All rubber seals were replaced and the leaks stopped. Such persistent efforts began to show results and the defect rate of the aircraft began to fall. Concurrently, the material state of the aircraft also improved with the policy of repair of major components by replacement. He also introduced a policy of not deferring a defect but rectifying it as and when it occurred. This eliminated most deferred defects on aircraft and especially those that placed a limitation on the aircraft's performance.

The material state of all aircraft improved. The morale and the confidence of the squadron's engineering personnel grew with it. The aircrew too began to see the change because the aircraft stayed serviceable and available for flying for a longer time.

No doubt this had an overall bearing on the availability of aircraft for operations during the war. It has been recognized that during the 1971 war, no planned operational sortie of the Sea Hawks from INS *Vikrant* was cancelled for want of an aircraft.

Lt Shahdadpuri

Lt R. Shahdadpuri, ALO INAS 300, recalls those days on board INS *Vikrant* before, during and after the war[1]:

---

[1] All first-person accounts were shared with the authors over interviews.

I started my career with frontline squadron INAS 300, which is the *numero uno* air squadron of the Indian Navy. The year 1971 was a special year in my life. It gave me the opportunity to be actively engaged in a real war right at the start of my career. I was an electrical officer in the general navy. I had volunteered to join the naval aviation in 1970. I was accepted and sent for basic orientation course at the Naval Air Technical School [now renamed as Naval Institute of Aeronautical Technology] at INS Garuda, Cochin. On completion of training, I joined the Alizé squadron INAS 310 as deputy AEO.

I had served for three months in INAS 310 when I was transferred to Sea Hawk Squadron INAS 300 in May 1971 as the squadron's ALO. I took over from Lt M.B. Lele, who was on leave at the time. Lt Uttam Singh was the AEO of the squadron, but he too got transferred out within a month of my joining. The squadron was in a relaxed mode. INS *Vikrant* had developed a serious defect in one of her boilers and it was common knowledge that there would be no embarkation for the squadron on the carrier for the next three to four years.

But then things changed suddenly. INS *Vikrant* was to sail in spite of the defects in her boiler. This was a very bold decision and it altered the course of the Indo-Pak War of 1971. In my view, the significance of this decision has not received due recognition in historical accounts of the Indian Navy of that time.

The 300 Squadron was to go to Meenambakkam, the civil airport of Madras, to exercise and train with the *Vikrant* operating in the sea off Madras. The *Vikrant* was to sail from Bombay to Visakhapatnam. The aircrew were to ferry the squadron of Sea Hawks from Goa to Meenambakkam. The air technical personnel and the remaining aircrew of the squadron travelled from Goa to Cochin by train with the Squadron Mobile Equipment (SME) and joined the *Vikrant* at Cochin. Lt Gurnam Singh was appointed the new squadron AEO. This was a big relief to me as being the only air technical officer in the squadron, I was performing the duties of the AEO too, and it was turning out to be stressful.

The *Vikrant* sailed from Cochin and reached Madras. We disembarked at Madras port and proceeded to the airport by road. The aircraft had not yet arrived at Meenambakkam. We organized ourselves in the open at Meenambakkam airfield and prepared to receive the aircraft from Goa. Lt Gurnam Singh joined the squadron at Meenambakkam.

After necessary flying practice and exercises, all the six Sea Hawk aircraft of the squadron landed on board. This was my first appointment to an embarked frontline jet fighter squadron. Initially, I did not know many procedures and also struggled with finding my way around the big ship. I was now the departmental head (electrical) in the squadron and responsible for maintenance of all aircraft. I felt like a non-swimmer thrown in the deep end of the pool to learn how to swim. The Indian Navy's way to train officers is to entrust them with responsibility. The navy puts trust in its officers and men, and they seldom disappoint.

Our Squadron Commanding Officer, Lt Cdr S.K. Gupta, was a thorough professional and a gentleman. Soon, more Sea Hawks began to arrive on board. The number of Sea Hawks in the squadron began to increase from the six that had arrived in the first lot. The number gradually increased and became eight, and then 10, and so on until it reached an astounding figure of 18 Sea Hawks. By this time, we knew that it was not an ordinary sailing. We were in for real action.

Aircraft operations from the aircraft carrier are significantly different from their operations from the shore. Flying from an aircraft carrier demands special and precise flying skills. For an air technical officer too, there are challenges over and above the normal maintenance and defect rectification of the aircraft.

The space available in aircraft hangars on board a carrier is limited. With 18 Sea Hawks of our squadron, along with six Alizés of INAS 300 and two Alouettes, the hangar and the flight deck were crowded. Aircraft maintenance often requires positioning the aircraft at appropriate places for servicing. Sometimes engineers need to work on the aircraft undercarriage for which the aircraft needs to be put on jacks; some may need an engine lift and then engine replacement, while some aircraft may require working on wings involving the spread and fold operations, which need additional space around the aircraft. Some aircraft require a ground run to prove and certify the engine performance.

Time for aircraft maintenance and defect rectification is limited since the aircraft are needed for flying. What is needed is profound knowledge of the aircraft and its systems, skill and experience. The aircraft operations demand perfect understanding and coordination among the technical team, squadron duty officer and teams working on flight deck and hangar. No book can teach this. One learns from regular corrections and criticism from peers, subordinates and seniors. The option to not perform is not available.

Lt Gurnam and I were cabin mates on board. A bathroom cubicle was close to our cabin. Our work in the squadron went round the clock. We could manage only short naps of sleep, take quick showers and go to the hangar or flight deck as the case might be. Our cabin was not air conditioned and it became uncomfortably sultry and hot in there. We could not sleep well. Lt Gurnam slept on the upper bunk and I on the lower. He had excellent technical know-how. He noticed that there was an air conditioning duct passing through our cabin near the ceiling, but it did not have a discharge point in our cabin. He saw that the duct had an opening for the cabin, but it had been blocked by a metal plate fixed by some screws. He removed the screws and the plate.

The hole in the duct opened and cool air began to flow into our cabin, but only till the top bunk. It did not reach me at the lower bunk. There was no way the cool air could be directed at me. Lt Gurnam solved the problem in a jiffy. He tied a pyjama on the outlet in the duct and the two legs of the pyjama immediately bloated with the cool air flowing through them. He dangled the second one towards my lower bunk. We thus shared the cool air and the heat did not bother us thereafter. It was a much-needed respite and we could sleep.

Rear Admiral S.K. Gupta

Rear Admiral S.K. Gupta, the commanding officer of the Sea Hawk Squadron INAS 300, describes the fast-changing events from his own experience of that period:

Finally, on 30 July 1971, six Sea Hawks, with many deferred defects in their aircraft documents, were ferry flown by our pilots from Goa to Madras. It was monsoon. Less than half of these pilots were instrument rated! To make these aircraft serviceable for the ferry flight, the other Sea Hawks in the squadron were made 'Christmas trees' and heavily robbed! Essential spares, such as exhaust units and hot-end spares needed for the engines, were to be indented from the manufacturers in the UK. The manufacturing lines for these spares had closed years ago and these spares were to be specially manufactured for the Indian Navy and paid for in foreign exchange, which was a scarce resource and needed special dispensation for its release. With low priority given to the squadron, the Indian Navy had little choice except to resign itself to this situation. No one was sure if *Vikrant* and her fighter squadrons would play any worthwhile role in the event of an all-out war with our belligerent neighbour.

The month of August 1971 witnessed *Vikrant*, the mother ship, controlling Sea Hawks at sea off Madras. The ship-based crew were inexperienced and unfamiliar with procedures in live situations of controlling aircraft at sea. Despite this, attempts were made on 14 August 1971 for the jets to carry out rollers on deck. As always, the pilots were glad to exercise with *Vikrant* in furtherance of the great mutual bond that existed between them, built up over years. It is pertinent to mention that the naval headquarters had not authorized the embarkation, not even the flying trials. The carrier, given its speed limitations and poor state of workup, was considered unsafe for jet operation—a reason enough for the naval headquarters to not issue orders for embarkation. The squadron, too, had been disembarked over a year ago, and was not in trained condition to undertake the task of embarked flying. Chances were being taken, and should things have gone wrong, it was doubtful if there would have been someone mercifully holding your hand!

With seven Sea Hawks now ashore in Madras, four of them were arrested on board *Vikrant* on 17 August 1971. The fifth Sea Hawk was deck-landed the next day, en route Vizag. The carrier, with five Sea Hawks and Alizé aircraft embarked, then proceeded to Port Blair, arriving on 29 September 1971. There was embarked flying on just four days in the month of September. The good news was that the awaited hot-end spares of the Sea Hawk's Nene engine ordered from the UK had begun to arrive. This prospect kindled hopes that more Sea Hawks would become available, and they would arrive in Madras between September-end and October-end 1971.

This period also witnessed the arrival of experienced pilots joining the squadron—some on temporary duty—to augment the pilot strength commensurate with the frontline aircraft establishment of 20 Sea Hawks. Unfortunately, the relatively inexperienced Sea Hawk pilots had to be disembarked to return to Goa to make way for the experienced ones, now totalling 15 pilots on board. It did not take long for the new arrivals to get their hand back to flying the Sea Hawk whilst embarked. The war was imminent, and by mid-November 1971, the ships of the carrier battle group (*Vikrant* with escort ships) were ready for war in the Bay of Bengal.

By October-end in 1971, the officer and aircraft strength in 300 Squadron included 15 pilots, two technical officers, with two deputies and 18 Sea Hawks. One aircraft had made a very heavy landing while arresting on 30 October, and sheared off its port undercarriage. This damaged aircraft was kept on board. It provided the spares required to keep other 18 Sea Hawks serviceable.

From whatever angle it was viewed, the situation which appeared bad a few weeks earlier had turned around quite remarkably. With the run-down state of the squadron ashore for more than a year until September 1971 and thereafter, given that there were just 24 embarked flying days in four months, the squadron's performance was accident-free and consistent with delivering weapons accurately. This was made possible with the aircraft serviceability achieving 100 per cent target on all days of the conflict, and the pilots remaining fit to fly at all times.

Lt Gurnam Singh, the squadron AEO, was a good air engineer and a hard task master. Professionally, he had a profound understanding of the Sea Hawk aircraft and since his joining, the aircraft serviceability had steadily improved. With 18 Sea Hawks in the squadron, the AEO had some difficulties with the flight deck and other departments of the ship, who did not seem to share the quantum of the squadron's work and enthusiasm to hone up the aircraft for the forthcoming operations. They did not attach the same urgency to problems as the AEO and ALO did, and this resulted in loss of time; and there was an understandable disappointment and even frustration. The squadron took it seriously. The matter was resolved at senior level and the squadron's requests began to receive the needed priority, attention and support. In this way, every priority was accorded to get the ship and the squadrons operational.

With such an environment, there was enthusiasm all round, which was clearly visible and felt throughout the period of five months commencing 30 July 1971, and the final post-war disembarkation of squadrons on 6 January 1972.

Lt Cdr Ashwini Kumar Mehra, Lt Cdr Gulab Israni, Lt Cdr P.D. Sharma, Lt Cdr Ashok Sinha, Senior Pilot, Lt Cdr Yashwant Manohar Bhide, Lt Vinod Pasricha, Lt Raminder Singh Sodhi, Lt Inder Meet Singh Gill and Lt S.P. Singh were the officers transferred on temporary duty to INAS 300 for embarkation and flying duties during the war. They were transferred to the squadron in order to enhance the availability of trained and experienced pilots for operations.

INAS 310: The Alizé Anti-Submarine Squadron

Before the war began, the Alizés were posted in Cochin. They were then moved to Dabolim, Goa, from where they were deployed on board the *Vikrant* once it was decided that the ship wouldn't remain in the harbour for this war but would play an active role. Rear Admiral Gobind Singh was the AEO of INAS 310 till June 1971. He was a lieutenant at the time. He was at Goa but under transfer from the squadron to INS Hansa near Dabolim, Goa. He shared details about the preparation of INAS 310 with the authors:

It was the end of the year 1970, and we had left our mother ship *Vikrant* a few months earlier. The 310 Alizés squadron was based in Cochin since its inception in 1961. When Goa gained its independence, the airport in Dabolim was transferred to the Indian Navy. The 300 Squadron, operating from INS Hansa at the Air Force Station, Sulur, in Coimbatore, was moved to Goa in 1964, along with the NAS. Since that time, there were plans to move the 310 Squadron as well to INS Hansa. It was around this time in 1970 that Lt Cdr R.D. Dhir, the squadron commanding officer, decided to move the Alizé squadron from Cochin to Goa.

The permanent shift of INAS 310 from Cochin to Goa involved a change of base. As the squadron AEO, and also its store officer, I had the responsibility to pack up everything including the aircrew lockers and the squadron vehicles.

The naval headquarters had reduced the unit establishment of INAS 310 from six Alizés to four. The aircraft were to be made ready to move to Goa. The most important aspect of the INAS 310 Squadron operating from Cochin was the support system available for the aircraft maintenance. The naval store depot was located nearby. All our spares came from there. The only major maintenance organization of the naval aviation, NARO, was a kilometre away, across the runway. Goa did not have comparable support facilities for Alizés, and this was a concern. There was also a shortage of sailors' accommodation in Goa. INAS 310 was asked to reduce the number of sailors by transferring some to other units in Cochin before the squadron's shift to Goa.

While we were preparing to move to Goa, the commissioning of the INAS 330[2], the Sea King Squadron,

---

[2]In the late 1960s, the Indian Navy had acquired the British manufactured ASW helicopters called Sea Kings. These were formed into a squadron called INAS 330.

was scheduled for 17 April 1971, and we were to provide a platoon for the ceremony. After this event, we set about implementing our shift to Goa. INS *Kirpan* was tasked to take our SME from Cochin to Goa. The aircraft were to fly from Cochin to Dabolim.

At Goa, Alizés were accommodated in the Bellman hangar. Hansa transport section and the INAS 321 of Alouette helicopters also operated from the same hangar. The AED was close by, but it was dealing with the maintenance of the Alizé aircraft and its systems for the first time. It did not have the expertise of working on Alizé aircraft and was unable to provide meaningful maintenance support to the squadron. The AED of INS Hansa, too, neither had any experience of electronic and electrical equipment fitted on Alizé nor did it have the test facilities. The test benches for the DRAA-2A radar and other specialized equipment installed on Alizé were available only at NARO in Cochin.

Lt Cdr O.P. Laul, the lieutenant commander (operations) of the *Vikrant*, visited Hansa in June 1971. He brought the message that the navy was preparing for the possibility of going to war with Pakistan and the *Vikrant* would take part. INAS 310 was required to embark on the aircraft carrier along with the Sea Hawk Squadron INAS 300.

The airframe and engines of Alizés could be serviced at Goa, but the avionics needed to go to NARO in Cochin. Thus, three Alizés were sent to Cochin and one was left with Hansa AED for them to make it fly-worthy.

The *Vikrant* arrived at Goa, and the INAS 310 SME personnel and the aircrew embarked on board. Lt M.V. Paul, the new ALO, was to join in Cochin. I had received my transfer orders from the squadron to AED Hansa. I was to leave by June 1971 and Lt K.R. Chopra was to take over as the new AEO. Lt Cdr Dhir, the squadron CO, wanted the new AEO to double-bank with me. So I, too, embarked the

Vikrant in Goa and went to Cochin. My Deputy Lt A.B. Patil was retained in Hansa AED to ready the four Alizé.

In Cochin, I had the reverse task of gathering the manpower, which had been transferred out of the squadron when we moved to Goa. It was a difficult job but a directive from higher authorities helped. The three aircraft sent to NARO were ready. Lt M.V. Paul joined on board.

I would have liked to stay on in the squadron as the ship was going to war, but Lt Cdr Dhir, my CO, told me that I would have to go, as Lt Cdr D'Souza, the station air engineer officer of Hansa, had refused to let go of Lt Patil, and also the Alizé aircraft unless I was sent back to Hansa. So that was that. I collected my luggage and boarded a train to Goa.

Commodore M.V. Paul (Retd) was lieutenant in 1971 when he took over as the ALO of the INAS 310. He narrated his experiences of the time to the authors:

I was commissioned in the electrical branch of the Indian Navy on 10 February 1969 and underwent the orientation course at INS Valsura, Jamnagar, from February 1969 to February 1970. Thereafter, I served on board INS *Brahmaputra* and INS *Vikrant*. My area of responsibility included power generation and distribution, and maintenance of all electrical machinery, including arrester gear and aircraft lifts. In June 1971, I was appointed ALO of INAS 310, the anti-submarine aircraft Alizé squadron. I continued in that post till April 1973.

For surveillance of the seas, the Alizé aircraft needed to be fully serviceable in all aspects. The aircraft systems had defects and could not perform missions successfully. Almost 50 per cent of cables on the planes had either short-circuited or had low electric insulation. The only remedy was to change the connectors having multiple pins, but spare connectors were not available. Some plugs had deteriorated due to ageing. We analysed the reason for the insulation breakdown and found that the rubber washers inside the plug housing were burnt. We handcrafted washers from rubber sheets, making suitable holes, and serviced all the connectors.

The radar started to function normally. The aircrew tested it and found it to be performing well. The next problem was the stabilization system for the radar. I improvised a method by which the vertical gyro could be made stable for radar operation. Each aircraft returned with systems serviceable after every recce sortie. Occasionally, I flew in the aircraft to assess the performance of the aircraft systems myself.

The aircraft were flying without a diversion airfield. When an aircraft carrier operates in the open sea and carries out flying operations, its aircraft take off from the carrier and land back on it. There is always a possibility, however small, that an aircraft launched from the carrier develops a defect and cannot land back on the ship. A heavy storm could develop around the aircraft carrier, and the ship might not consider it safe to recover the aircraft. To cater to such situations, an airport on nearby land is normally nominated as diversion airfield for the aircraft of the aircraft carrier. Thus, if an aircraft that is airborne and cannot land back on carrier for one reason or the other, the ship diverts the aircraft to the nominated diversion airfield. The aircraft is later recovered on board when ready. Flying without such a diversion airfield removes the safety net for the aircraft.

It was, therefore, essential that navigation equipment of Alizés function satisfactorily, especially at night. With systems serviceable, Alizés performed their missions successfully, blocking all traffic to and from East Pakistan and rounding up clandestine ships and directing them to Paradip Harbour. Night bombing sorties of the aircraft were successful, though on one occasion, one Alizé suffered bullet hits from enemy anti-aircraft gunfire. Alizés contributed substantially in establishing sea control in the Bay of Bengal. While the Sea Hawks struck ships, installations and other assets of military value in Cox's Bazar, Khulna and Chittagong, Alizés joined them to establish total control of the seas. I was awarded the Nao Sena Medal for my contribution to the war effort.

Operating from INS *Vikrant*, Alizé aircraft mounted intensive strikes on East Pakistan from 4 December 1971 onwards, and flew over 291 sorties in 10 days. Alizés carried out mining of the areas around the ports of East Pakistan and bombed Pakistani ships, preferably at night to avoid combat with enemy aircraft. On 5 December, the Alizés detected a Pakistani Daphné-class submarine and forced it to surface with anti-submarine charges, and attacked it with rockets. Alizés conducted bombing raids and rocket attacks on ships anchored in Pakistani ports in the east.

The Vikrant Goes to War

Recalling the *Vikrant*'s deployment in the Bay of Bengal in 1971, Admiral S.M. Nanda, the then CNS, wrote:

> Between August and October 1971, the Carrier Task Group worked itself up to a high state of operational readiness off Madras and Visakhapatnam and also in Andaman and Nicobar Islands. These islands provided excellent natural, deep-water, sheltered and secret anchorages away from prying eyes and constrained harbours of the mainland. Our plan was to use these anchorages in the event of war. Our intelligence inputs alerted us to Pakistan's plan to stalk and sink the *Vikrant*, the pride of Indian Navy, by using one of its submarines. In fact, our assessment had revealed that only submarine Ghazi had the adequate endurance to be deployed

off the east coast of India, and we were to be proved correct.

The growing operational activity in the eastern theatre made it necessary to upgrade the command-and-control structure, so that the commanding officers of ships were not detracted from their primary duties. The naval headquarters gave orders for the Eastern Fleet to be formally constituted on 1 November 1971, with Rear Admiral Harilal Sarma at its helm. INS *Vikrant*, the two Brahmaputra-class escort ships, INS *Brahmaputra* and *Beas*, the two Petya-class corvettes, Kamorta and Kavaratti, and the submarine Khanderi were assigned to him.

Vikrant was to be the key to controlling the Bay of Bengal and denying all seaward logistical and material sustenance to East Pakistan. While, on the one hand, operational plans required that an area of approximately 18,000 sq. miles be kept under surveillance, on the other, it was necessary to commit the entire striking power of *Vikrant*'s aircraft to offensive operations against enemy ships and installations. Also, the areas of operation between the Air Force and the Navy had to be demarcated. The ports of Chittagong, Cox's Bazar and the Chalna-Khulna-Mongla river ports complex, were particularly targeted.

Vikrant was the pivot of all maritime operations in the eastern theatre of war. Its aircraft performed a variety of tasks: they complemented the IAF air operations, neutralized targets of maritime importance ashore and afloat; established control over contraband; and helped in the early capitulation of the Pakistani forces in the eastern wing. *Vikrant* acquitted itself with flying colours during the 1971 war, much to the disbelief of the doubting Thomases.[3]

On 2 December 1971, the Eastern Fleet proceeded to its patrol

---

[3]Nanda, S.M., *The Man Who Bombed Karachi: A Memoir*, HarperCollins Publishers India, 2015, pp. 203–05.

area in the north of the Bay of Bengal in anticipation of an attack by Pakistan. The hostilities broke out on 3 December 1971. By then, the *Vikrant* had closed in on the East Pakistan port city of Chittagong. In the forenoon of 4 December, the Sea Hawk jet fighters struck enemy shipping in Chittagong and Cox's Bazar harbours, striking, sinking and severely damaging most of the ships in the two ports.

On 4 December, 3,000 km from Karachi to the east, by first light, the Eastern Naval Fleet of the Indian Navy positioned itself in the waters of the Bay of Bengal, within air striking range of East Pakistan. In the next few hours, as the day progressed, INS *Vikrant* launched wave after wave of her Sea Hawk jet fighters to attack the ports and cities of East Pakistan. In the following days, the *Vikrant* continued to launch specific missions of its Sea Hawk jet fighters and the anti-submarine Alizé aircraft to bomb, rocket attack and cannon strafe strategic assets and targets in East Pakistan. The Indian Navy delivered yet another powerful blow of a missile attack on Karachi on 8 December, causing further devastation and widespread destruction of the Pakistan naval fleet warships in Karachi harbour, oil storage depots and other significant naval support and maintenance infrastructure.

Over the next few days, Sea Hawks launched from the *Vikrant* struck targets in Khulna and the Mongla ports, and destroyed strategic enemy assets and installations. On 14 December, the Sea Hawks from INS *Vikrant* attacked the army cantonment in Chittagong with guns, bombs and rockets. Many Pakistani army barracks, power houses, storehouses and installations were destroyed and damaged. During their attacks, the *Vikrant*'s Sea Hawks faced gunfire from the Pakistani anti-aircraft gun positions. Alizés continued their attacks on Cox's Bazar, a coastal town of East Pakistan where enemy troop concentration was reported. By this time, Pakistani forces had stopped retaliation. After carrying out the attack by Sea Hawks on East Pakistan on 14 December, the *Vikrant* had completed the fleet's task substantially. The *Vikrant* was now running low on fuel, so she sailed to the port of Paradip on the eastern coast for refuelling.

The Eastern Fleet was formally constituted on 1 November 1971. All the ships sailed for Andaman and Nicobar Islands on 13 November 1971. For security reasons, the *Vikrant* sailed to a remote anchorage. Simultaneously, deception signals were generated that gave the impression that the *Vikrant* was operating from a location between Madras and Visakhapatnam. On the night of 3 December, the naval coastal battery at Visakhapatnam heard an explosion. The next day, a diving team was sent down to search the area. The divers found the Pakistani submarine PNS Ghazi lying on the seabed in a seriously damaged condition. The Ghazi had sunk in shallow waters.

Two Defects and Their Solutions

The operation and achievements of the *Vikrant* are even more remarkable considering the fact that she was an old ship. The *Vikrant* wasn't in top shape. Two incidents illustrate the point that the *Vikrant* was showing signs of age and significant defects in critical systems had started to manifest themselves. The first occurred just before the war and the second in the last couple of days of the war.

A serious defect in the ship's tracking radar showed itself in October 1971 when the ship was committed to play an active and offensive role in the anticipated war with Pakistan in the Bay of Bengal. In fact, as the events unfolded, the war was only five weeks away. The *Vikrant* and her aircraft squadrons were destined to play a memorable and historical role in the weeks ahead, perhaps the most important of their lives. The defect and how it was rectified was shared by Commodore Gurbachan Singh Kanwal, who was a lieutenant at the time.

The month of September 1971 had just ended. INS *Vikrant*, accompanied by the warships of the carrier battle group, had been conducting war games and carrying out flying exercises in the Bay of Bengal in the seas between Visakhapatnam and Andaman and Nicobar Islands. It was during such flying operations that an unforeseen situation began to develop in the ship.

The functioning of the ship's long-range aircraft warning radar, called Type 960 Radar, was the main radar of *Vikrant*. It gave the ship the capability of looking at a distance of about 200 nautical miles and tracking the bearing and range of an aircraft at that distance. It tracked the airspace around the ship for friendly and non-friendly aircraft within its detection range. Radar 963, the second radar in the ship, functioned as the secondary radar, with a range of 40 nautical miles. This important radar became erratic on occasions.

With the main radar becoming defective, the ship could not be put to sea, as she would not be able to detect an aircraft approaching her and determine if it was a friend or a foe. The ship's own safety was at risk and compromised. Also, the ship was not able to track her own aircraft and guide them to the ship when they were shipward bound after completion of their flying mission. The main radar was, thus, crucial for the carrier to undertake aircraft operations of both Sea Hawks and Alizés in the Bay of Bengal.

The *Vikrant* was brought to Madras to work on the defect, but the ship remained on 24-hour notice to sail out of the harbour. The ship couldn't stay longer for a number of reasons. There was a constant threat to the *Vikrant* from the Pakistan Navy submarine Ghazi, which was suspected to be in the Bay of Bengal, looking for the *Vikrant*. The carrier was, therefore, kept moving, so as to change its location and thus avoid detection by the Ghazi. Also, the port of Madras was a large seaport with merchant ships loading and unloading, and a large human traffic and presence. This constituted a security threat to the *Vikrant*. The ship had to remain ready to move out of the harbour at short notice in case of any eventuality. The ship's boilers remained lit and steaming.

The ship's staff inspected the radar and concluded that it was beyond their capability to repair the defect.

Specialized and expert help was available only on the western coast in the Naval Dockyard at Bombay, the home port of the *Vikrant*, where WECORS workshop, specializing in the weapon equipment and the Radar 960 installation on board the *Vikrant* was located. A repair team of one officer and about seven civilian radar specialists from the WECORS workshop was constituted. The team was led by Lt Gurbachan Singh Kanwal, an electrical officer with professional expertise, to solve such difficult operational problems.

On request from Indian Navy, an IAF AN-12 aircraft flew Lt Kanwal and his team to Madras. Some components of the Radar 960 system were defective and needed replacement. They had bought some spare parts with them. They were suitable but their dimensions did not match with the unserviceable parts to be replaced and they had to be machined to make their dimensions suitable.

Around this time, the *Vikrant* had to sail for operational reasons. The repair work was stopped and the team was disembarked. The *Vikrant* returned to Madras a few days later and the WECORS team completed the work in early November 1971. This important defect in the ship's main radar that affected the ship's operational capability was rectified just a few days before the war broke out.

The second incident was perhaps more serious and took place on the last day of the war. The ship's steam catapult and the aircraft arresting system for landing on board are the prime responsibilities of the flight deck engineer officer (FDEO) and his department. He is also responsible for the two aircraft lifts that take the aircraft from the hangar to the flight deck or from the flight deck to the hangar. The lifts work round the clock.

On 14 December 1971, the war was nearly over. The *Vikrant* was still in the operational area in the north of the Bay of Bengal, off Dacca. She was left with 25 per cent of the fuel and was ordered to proceed to refuel at Paradip Harbour. On the way, the *Vikrant* carried out aircraft flying. Four Sea Hawks had been launched and were due for recovery on board when the aft aircraft lift of the *Vikrant* developed a defect. The aft lift formed a part of the flight deck when it was fully up and level with the flight deck. The aircraft arrestor wires passed over the aft lift. But now, the lift was stuck 2 ft below, creating a square well in the flight deck.

This meant that the aircraft that were in the air could not be recovered. It was an emergency situation. The engineers were trying their best to raise the lift to make it level with the flight deck.

The engineering team did not succeed in making the lift travel up and level with the flight deck. It was time for the ship to recover the aircraft that had been launched, but they could not be recovered till the aft lift was levelled with the flight deck. The ship's Commander (Air) and his team were in a state of panic. If, in the next few minutes, the lift did not level with the flight deck and the arrestor wires were not stretched across the flight deck, the aircraft, which were in the air, would run out of fuel and the pilots would have to ditch their aircraft in the sea. The situation was becoming graver with the passing of every moment. The pilots would have to eject from the aircraft before ditching them. They would have to be picked up from the sea. The *Vikrant* began to prepare for the worst.

Capt. Parkash was informed. He came down from the bridge to the flight deck to check the problem. The FDEO and his team were desperate. They made a last-ditch effort. They took the aft lift back down to the hangar level. The lift had two large electric motors to move the lift up and down. The power and the capacity of one motor was enough to move the lift up or down even when loaded with an aircraft. The FDEO ordered both the motors to be started and engaged.

The lift began to move up. With double the power now available, the lift speeded up, and when it reached near the top, it struck the keep lock, broke it with a loud bang and went up to complete its full travel. It had levelled with the flight deck but not before giving goosebumps to everyone on the ship. The arrestor wires could now be stretched to recover the aircraft. All the aircraft were recovered on board safely. After this incident, instructions were issued to permanently keep the aft lift level with the flight deck and locked in that position.

Looking back at the incident half a century later, one can only say that it was good fortune that this incident happened when the war had all but come to an end. Had it happened a few days earlier, when there was intensive flying taking place from the *Vikrant* during the war, and multiple launches and recoveries of aircraft were going on round the clock, with the aircraft lifts working constantly to move the aircrafts from hangar to flight deck and vice-versa, it would have seriously dented the *Vikrant's* war effort.

There were other difficult situations faced by the squadron because of the age of the Sea Hawk aircraft. The defects appeared with unpredictable frequency, and the squadron engineering team and the logistic experts on board had to cope with those. The squadron's engineering team had to find solutions fast, always prioritizing the safety of the aircrew and the aircraft first.

≈

9

Some Notes from the War

There are a few things from the war days that capture the flavour of the life and activities on board the *Vikrant* and its squadrons, before and during the operations till 16 December 1971 when Pakistan signed the surrender document.[1]

9 November 1971

The *Vikrant* was operating in the Bay of Bengal in the sea between Madras and Visakhapatnam. There was a feeling that the war was not too far away. All reports and the general buzz indicated that war was now imminent. On 9 November, the day for the squadrons started with a launch of nine Sea Hawks and three Alizés for a fly-past in honour of the President of India. The weather was calm with no wind conditions prevailing. The Sea Hawks returned with a report that there was a belt, about half a mile wide, within which there were favourable wind conditions. The carrier was operating in this belt. It explained why there was wind on deck permitting take-offs and landings. On either

---

[1]These notes are compiled from the journals the authors maintained during the war.

side of this belt, there was hardly any wind. The ship and the squadrons were happy that the wind on deck allowed to meet the commitment to stage the fly-past in honour of President V.V. Giri, who was visiting Madras.

The weather off Visakhapatnam remained cool and crisp. It would get cold at night, so one would require a cover at night and early morning. The ship's engineers were kind and provided hot water in the showers, which was quite welcome. INS *Brahmaputra* and INS *Beas* were sailing with the *Vikrant*.

We listened attentively to the news from the All India Radio (AIR), but there was not much in it. The work in the squadrons kept us busy and occupied from early morning to late night.

10-13 November 1971

The *Vikrant* was outside Madras and flew on 10 November. She entered the harbour on the morning of 11. The sky was covered with grey clouds with a forecast for rain. As the *Vikrant* was entering the harbour, a heavy downpour greeted us. The weatherman told us it was due to a low-pressure area over the city. The weather remained grey and wet for the next two days and the skies cleared only on the morning of 13 November. The squadron utilized this two-day break to catch up with maintenance work on our Sea Hawks. The Sea Hawks arriving from Hansa had many deferred defects that were entered in the Aircraft Form A-700.

The squadron welcomed the aircraft as they built the aircraft numbers. As soon as they arrived, the AEO and his teams scrutinized the aircraft documents and started focusing on rectifying all the deferred defects. The AEO followed the policy of keeping the limitations and deferred defects log of the aircraft clean. The aircrew welcomed his approach.

The ship sailed out and commenced flying. The last two Sea Hawks joining the squadron were recovered on board. The squadron now had a full unit establishment of 18 Sea Hawks embarked. One Sea Hawk's stub wing was damaged because of the heavy landing. It was parked permanently in the C hangar of the *Vikrant*. Including the damaged aircraft, there were 19 Sea Hawks on board. The old hands told us that this was the highest frontline aircraft establishment of Sea Hawks ever held on board *Vikrant*. It was a great feeling to see so many Sea Hawks on board. It filled the ship and the squadron with pride. The flight deck handlers' team of the ship's air department had a tough time managing the movements and parking of so many Sea Hawks on the flight deck and the hangar. Soon after the two Sea Hawks landed on board, the *Vikrant* set course for Andaman and Nicobar Islands.

15 November 1971

The *Vikrant* was sailing through an area of clean and crisp wind. The sea had a greenish-blue colour. It was a pleasure to come up to the flight deck to look at the sea and breathe in the fresh and invigorating air. The squadron was observing an aircraft cleaning day. It had 14 serviceable Sea Hawks; the other four were under routine maintenance and defect rectification. The squadron was looking forward to intensive flying. A flying programme of 40 launches was released for 16 November.

16 November 1971

The first launch in the morning had to be cancelled. The aft lift became unserviceable and the aircraft could not be moved as per the flying programme for the day. The serviceable Sea Hawk aircraft could not be brought up from the aircraft hangars to the flight deck in time for their before-flight inspections for the first launch scheduled for 5.30 a.m. The Air Department made every effort, but the situation did not come under control. The haste resulted in some near-miss situations for both the aircraft and the men. There were lessons learnt all round.

17 November 1971

The *Vikrant* was at Port Blair, the capital of Andaman and Nicobar Islands in the Bay of Bengal. It was a very beautiful place, bright and clear in the November sun. The squadron utilized the time in the harbour for maintenance and defect rectification of aircraft.

18 November 1971

The *Vikrant* was anchored in the outer harbour of Port Blair. The squadron had been working hard for the last few weeks and the strain began to show. The Sea Hawk was an old aircraft and the effects of age were evident. The aircraft needed more maintenance to keep them fit for flying, and their systems needed closer and deeper inspections to catch defects in the early stages. The squadron maintenance policy, followed by the AEO was to catch such defects and rectify them before they manifested. With hard work, the aircraft availability improved significantly, and it continued to improve and surprise the squadron most pleasantly.

19-20 November 1971

It was a pleasant morning. The squadron personnel went for a walk and a run to get some exercise. The weather and exercise did everyone a lot of good and they returned to the ship in a happy and joyful mood.

21 November 1971

Lt Gurnam Singh (AEO), Lt Shahdadpuri (ALO), and some aircrew members organized a picnic for the squadron sailors and took them to Corbyn's Cove, a picturesque spot in the islands. The sailors threw some of their seniors into the water with their clothes on. Everyone enjoyed themselves. Once the picnic was over, they walked back to the jetty in the pleasant warm sun. They sang songs, picked up pebbles and shells on the way and spent a carefree and happy afternoon. The fresh sea breeze blowing in their faces brought them closer to nature. It was a happy way of de-stressing. Some visited Ross Island, which used to be the house of the British chief commissioner in the pre-Independence days. The island was about half a mile from Port Blair town and the Naval Garrison operated from there. Some visited the Cellular Jail where the freedom fighters were incarcerated in inhumane conditions by the British government ruling India at the time. There were gruesome gallows where those sentenced to death were hanged.

22 November 1971

The *Vikrant* was at Andaman and Nicobar Islands. Each new day welcomed us with fresh cool winds and blue seas. The islands around were rich in natural beauty and splendour—perhaps the best of the tropics. The squadron was refreshed after a visit to these islands and was ready for another outing to the sea for flying. We were looking forward to an intensive flying workup at sea. There was little work to be done because of the hangar rounds by the Captain. The squadron was focusing on sprucing up the aircraft for the Captain's rounds.

We heard that Pakistan Navy had put out its fleet to sea to head for the East Pakistani ports, a journey of about 1,600 nautical miles.

The BBC reported that two brigades of the Indian Army had crossed into East Pakistan and there had been an armed engagement. Four Pakistani Sabre aircraft had flown over Indian territory. Gnats of the IAF had challenged them and shot down one Sabre. There was a smell of war in the air. The squadron engineers were focussed on maximum availability of the aircraft.

23 November 1971

The weather continued to be excellent and the morale of the squadron was high. The men worked efficiently and cheerfully in the November sunshine. The afternoon news from AIR reported that three Pakistani Sabre jets had been shot down over Indian territory and pilots of two had been captured. Two Indian brigades had marched across the Jessore sector and the Indian thrust in the East had also begun. There was also the news that the Pakistani fleet was at sea and Pakistan had declared a national emergency.

24 November 1971

The drums of war had begun to roll in the eastern sector. A night before, the men of the duty watches transferred ammunition and supplies from INS *Gharial* into the ship. The ship sailed at 8.00 a.m. and carried out a full day's flying en route, using Port Blair as diversion airfield. The flying was good. The serviceability and availability of the aircraft made the squadron feel satisfied with the day's work.

There was news that the Indian Army has destroyed 15 Pakistani tanks in the eastern sector. The Pakistan fleet was reported to be at sea with one cruiser, four destroyers and one submarine. Everyone listened to news bulletins whenever they got an opportunity.

25 November 1971

We were in Port Cornwallis, a protected natural harbour in the north of the Andaman Islands. It consisted of one entrance from the open sea, which led to a large lagoon. In this location, the ships were concealed from view.

The squadron engineers continued their work on the flight deck and in the hangars. The squadron integrated itself into a hardworking, confident and efficient team. The relationship between officers and men was healthy. We were all on the same frequency, functioning as an efficient and disciplined unit. One could call it a lean and mean machine. It was necessary to give our men as much rest as possible. There was a long period of hard work ahead. But it was difficult to tell this to the AEO and the ALO, who were ever focussed on their priorities. Rest was far from their minds.

27 November 1971

There was a tug of war match between the Air Department and the squadron. For this, the opposite team fielded the strongest and heaviest of their men. Our squadron team consisted of lean men with lithe bodies, strong from hard work but with little body mass. We were nervous for our team after looking at our tough opponents. Our morale was high and our men knew that the squadron had to win this tournament.

When the whistle was blown, both teams began to pull at the rope. The rest of the squadron cheered loudly but to our disappointment, the rope moved some distance towards the Air Department. The entire squadron cheered and shouted, and asked our team to hold steady. This enthused our team and injected fresh energy into them. They pulled with increased vigour. There was a pause of a few moments and then the rope slowly moved towards us. We were going to win.

But our opponents made a last-ditch effort and the rope stopped a little short of the winning line. The aircrew and entire squadron were cheering our team. The team made another big effort and it was over. Our squadron had won. We went wild with jubilation.

28 November 1971

The Captain spoke to the ship's company on the ship's broadcast system. He said that matters were stirring up in East Pakistan, and the action could begin in two to four days' time. Till then, the *Vikrant* and other accompanying ships were to remain at the anchorage.

A concert was put up by our squadron, Engine Room and Air Department. We were the first to go on stage and as usual, the boys carried the show. Chief Uniyal, an accomplished singer, played the harmonium too. Everyone enjoyed our performance and complimented us.

29 November 1971

The squadron was working as a team with enthusiasm and zeal. It was cool and working on deck was quite pleasant. The aircraft serviceability state rose to 16 out of 18 aircraft, and the AEO said the other two aircraft would be ready soon.

30 November 1971

The BBC and the Voice of America reported the beginning of thrust by the Indian forces. American President Richard Nixon had written to Pakistan President Yahya Khan, who kept making noises, accusing India of an undeclared war. Pakistan was approaching its friends in the West for an intervention. Pakistan was scared.

The squadron arranged a tea party in the hangar. The squadron Master Chief Aircraft Artificer, Sampath Kumar, was very pleased to say a few words on the occasion.

Senior Pilot Lt Cdr Ashok Sinha also spoke to the men and appreciated the hard work being put in by everyone and the excellent aircraft serviceability in the squadron. The men were happy and cheerful. There was a deep sense of coherence and togetherness in the squadron.

1 December 1971

The morning started off with 'action stations' at 7.00 a.m. for half an hour. Action stations is a high state of readiness of a warship. When a warship gets ready to mount an attack or if she expects an attack or perceives a threat, she assumes action stations. It ensures maximum state of readiness of the warship. When 'action stations' is announced on a ship's broadcast, everyone on the ship is to go to the spot and post allocated to him as his duty station. It does not matter at what time of the day or night the announcement is made. It must be obeyed immediately.

Since we were at war and the *Vikrant* was launching its jet fighters for an attack, she assumed action stations. The first launch of Sea Hawks was scheduled for 11.00 a.m.

A serious accident was averted. Naval Airman D. Singh was blasted off the deck by jet blast of the aircraft in front. He did not fall overboard and got away with minor cuts and bruises.

All squadron pilots were able to fly. One of our aircraft experienced total electrical failure and was diverted ashore. A helicopter was taking the ALO, the AEO and their men ashore to Nicobar to service the aircraft. The aircraft was expected to be ready by sunrise. Our CO, Lt Cdr S.K. Gupta, planned to go ashore by the ship's helicopter early in the morning and fly the aircraft back on board. Later, a helicopter was to bring back the AEO, ALO and their team.

2 December 1971

The ship was put to sea. It was decided to fly only a couple of launches in the morning and then depart for our area of operation. However, once the rhythm of flying was established, the Captain decided to continue flying. It was a good decision because all the squadron aircrew were able to fly at least one sortie each. The display of professional competence and performance of the squadron's technical team and the aircrew demonstrated high professional standards. The performance of the squadron went like clockwork. The aircraft did not fail, nor did the aircrew. The air department and the flight deck teams worked efficiently with good results.

The squadron was going to see action and welcomed the opportunity. The aircrew and technical officers were in high spirits. The Captain addressed the ship's company late the previous night over the ship's broadcast. He said the *Vikrant* and the carrier battle group would be at war once the ships left Port Cornwallis.

Later, the *Vikrant* sailed out to open sea for flying off Port Blair. On completion of flying, the ship returned to Port Cornwallis on Ross Island to pick up the rest of the fleet. The *Vikrant* also collected some stores from the landing ship INS *Guldar*. She had come from Visakhapatnam to make deliveries to the *Vikrant*. We sailed from Port Cornwallis late at night.

3 December 1971

At about 7.15 p.m., the Captain addressed the ship's company over the ship's broadcast system. He was crisp and clear. He announced that India had declared hostilities against Pakistan. Everyone stood where he was and listened. It was clear that what lay ahead was the war itself. The Captain's speech lifted the spirits of the ship's company. In the squadron, there was a sense of renewed confidence and determination. The *Vikrant* and her squadrons would go into action to destroy the enemy. The ship was going to remain at 'flying stations' round the clock now. Unlike the Sea Hawks that do not have a radar and, therefore, operate only during the day, the Alizés were equipped with a radar and could operate at night. The *Vikrant* and all the accompanying ships of the carrier battle group were darkened completely at night for the fear of detection by the enemy submarine that may be lurking.

The 9.00 p.m. news from AIR reported that Pakistan had attacked Srinagar, Pathankot and Amritsar on the Western Front.

4 December 1971

It was the most memorable day for the Sea Hawk squadron. There was hardly anyone in the squadron who had had proper sleep for the last two nights. The squadron awoke early. The aircrew closed up for Carrier Airborne Patrol from dawn onwards. The squadron aircraft were ready to strike. A strike of eight Sea Hawks on Cox's Bazar was planned for 10.30 a.m. There was a quiet determination and excitement on the ship.

Captains of the ships in company of the *Vikrant* sent to the squadron their messages of goodwill and 'good hunting'. Our Captain said, 'This is the first time the aircrew are going to fire their weapons in anger.' He also briefed the aircrew and wished them luck. Cameras were clicking all around to record the historic moments.

Lt Cdr S.K. Gupta, our squadron CO, led the first strike of four Sea Hawks. It was followed by another four Sea Hawks, led by the squadron's senior pilot Lt Cdr Ashok Sinha. The other three with the senior pilot were Lt S.P. Singh, Lt Cdr Gulab Israni and Lt Prem Kumar. The Cox's Bazar airfield, the power house, two electric transformers and the Air Traffic Control of Cox's Bazar were struck by rockets. Strafing by the front guns of the Sea Hawks destroyed the installations and vehicles on the runway and set them on fire. After expending their ammunition, the eight Sea Hawks returned to the ship safely.

The squadron and ship's personnel greeted the aircrew enthusiastically as they stepped out of their aircraft after landing on board. The men lifted the squadron commander and other aircrew on their shoulders, and the roar of the White Tigers rent the air. Everyone's morale on the *Vikrant* was sky-high. The White Tigers of the Sea Hawk squadron were operational. There was relief that all our aircraft launched for the attack had returned safely to the ship. Congratulations kept pouring in and everyone in the squadron felt a sense of pride.

The *Vikrant* planned a second strike by the Sea Hawks in the afternoon. INS *Brahmaputra* picked up a submarine contact with the *Beas* and *Kamorta* in company. The *Kamorta* fired her anti-submarine rockets on the position at which the contact was reported. We learnt later that some oil was seen on the water and distress signals were intercepted. These showed that the submarine was hit and damaged. The ships did not stop to investigate the incident.

The submarine episode delayed the next launch of eight Sea Hawks by about 45 minutes. The strike was launched at 3.15 p.m. instead of at 2.30 p.m. The aircraft attacked the Chittagong airfield, the harbour installations and ships alongside the jetties. Later, there were reports that smoke was rising from many sites in Chittagong and that the widespread damage and destruction in the city from the attacks by the Sea Hawks were plainly visible.

All eight aircraft of the afternoon strike returned safely to the *Vikrant*. There was a joyous welcome from the squadron and the ship's company, with a repeat of the scenes from the morning. The officers' anteroom was full of excitement and laughter in the evening. There was a good-hearted bonhomie all around. The ship, the squadron, the aircrew and the engineers were satisfied with the day's performance. It was a job well done.

5 December 1971

Contrary to the day before, 5 December was a day of disappointments. Sea Hawks were to attack Chittagong early in the morning. The ports of Chalna, Khulna and Mongla were to be struck in the afternoon, but the day opened with grey weather and overcast skies. There was an atmospheric depression in the area and the wind had dropped to 3 to 4 knots. The *Vikrant* could not launch fully-armed Sea Hawks with such low wind speeds on the flight deck. The squadron waited the whole day without any luck.

At night, Alizés bombed the ports of Chalna, Khulna and Mongla. Alizés do not have hard points on their wings to carry these bombs. They carry them loose and hand-launch them over the targets. Sea Hawks were scheduled to move in next morning for strikes. There was good news from the western seaboard. All India Radio reported that Indian Navy's missile attack on Karachi had sunk three Pakistani ships on the west coast. One Pakistani warship *Shah Jahan* had been hit and badly damaged.

6 December 1971

The *Vikrant* launched a strike of 10 Sea Hawks and two Alizés at dawn to attack the ports of Chalna, Mongla and Khulna. Lt Cdr Ashwin Mehra and Lt Cdr Gulab Israni led these strikes. One Sea Hawk was hit by bullets from the enemy anti-aircraft gunfire. The strike in Mongla reaped rich dividends. The place was full of enemy gunboats and anti-aircraft gun batteries. The Sea Hawks attacked a gun boat and a tug with rockets, scoring direct hits and damaging them badly. The Sea Hawks strafed six or seven crafts with their front guns and continued the attack on three more gunboats. One gunboat was severely damaged and put out of action. The other two caught fire and began to burn with smoke billowing from them. During this attack, the Sea Hawks encountered heavy anti-aircraft gunfire from the Pakistani gunboats, but the aircraft managed to avoid getting hit.

The Sea Hawks spotted a merchant ship at a jetty and attacked it with rockets, damaging it. Some shore installations were also attacked. The aircraft spotted and strafed two more gunboats, putting them out of action. A wireless transmission station and a cargo ship were also attacked and damaged severely.

In the afternoon, Lt Pasricha led three aircraft to Hathazari. The squadron senior pilot, Lt Cdr Ashok Sinha, led another three Sea Hawks to attack Dohazari. They were tasked to look for airstrips and military installations, attack them and put them out of action. They did not find any airstrip. They then carried out an attack on Chittagong. They noticed a merchant ship some distance away from the coast and attacked it, causing severe damage.

The ship launched the last strike of the day to attack Chittagong once again. The Sea Hawks attacked and blew up two Pakistani fuel dumps, the naval base of Pakistan Navy and some installations. It was a rewarding and satisfying day for the squadron.

Alizés were launched for reconnaissance and strikes on merchant vessels near Pusur River. On completion of successful strikes on ships, the Alizé aircraft attacked the wireless station on the west bank of Pusur and destroyed it. A report was received in the evening that senior officials of Pakistani armed forces would be evacuated by air from Chittagong by midnight. One Alizé aircraft carried out bombing over Cox's Bazar and two Alizés bombed Chittagong airfield.

7 December 1971

It started getting colder, especially at nights. The wind picked up during the night but faded in the afternoon. The day was different than usual, as the wind stayed the entire time. The *Vikrant* launched two Sea Hawks in the morning to strike Cox's Bazar. Four Sea Hawks were launched to attack Chittagong again. The objective was to attack and damage the runways in both these places to render the airports unusable for take-off and landing of aircraft. The objectives were achieved.

8 December 1971

It was an uneventful day with no Sea Hawk flying. The AEO was focusing his attention on the aircraft that were damaged by the Pakistani anti-aircraft gunfire. He and his team were working round the clock to repair the damage, although such repair could be undertaken only at repair yards. It was heartening to see these attempts of repairing the aircraft to make them serviceable again for flying duties.

9 December 1971

A launch of eight Sea Hawks was planned for the morning. It was delayed by an hour because a convoy of ships was sighted nearby. INS *Kavaratti* and INS *Beas* were detached to investigate and apprehend them. On approaching the convoy, the *Beas* asked them to disclose their identity and ordered them to steer a particular course. They disobeyed. The *Beas* opened fire, sinking two of them. Soon after, the rest obeyed, and the *Beas* and *Kavaratti* escorted them to Paradip Port, south of the eastern coast. It was a new port in Orissa (now Odisha), on the eastern coast of India. It was about 60 miles from both Bhubaneswar and Cuttack, the two important cities of the state of Orissa. The survivors from the ships that were hit and sunk were picked up. Further investigations revealed that the two ships were carrying Pakistani troops.

The FOC-in-C East ordered the *Vikrant* to attack Barishal. Two Alizés were launched for the strike with bombs. Twenty minutes later, four Sea Hawks were launched to continue the attack on Barishal. Sea Hawks attacked an army camp and seven cargo barges. The camp was damaged heavily and three barges were destroyed. The Pakistanis were on the run.

In the afternoon, the Alizés attacked one tanker and damaged it. A strike of Sea Hawks on Chittagong was launched. The aircraft met heavy ground fire, and one Sea Hawk was hit by anti-aircraft bullets. The aircraft experienced total hydraulic failure. The aircrew managed to control the aircraft and brought it back to land on ship.

We learnt of the destruction of the Pakistani submarine Ghazi. Divers found bodies of Pakistanis inside the Ghazi. The front portion of the submarine was found to have been blown away. The markings confirmed the identity of the sunk submarine. She was killed by INS *Rajput*. This was creditable because INS *Rajput* did not have a sonar and had carried out the attack on the submarine following visual signals.

The *Vikrant* now had only one ship, *Kavaratti*, for company. Others had been detached from the carrier battle group to escort captured ships or to refuel themselves at Paradip. The Sea Hawks did not fly due to insufficient wind on the flight deck.

It was morning when the *Vikrant* passed a Greek ship. It had been abandoned by its crew after an attack by our Sea Hawks, and left to drift. The damage to the ship from our air attacks was visible from a distance. Holes made by shells from the front gun strafing by Sea Hawks could also be seen. The attack on the ship had knocked out the engine room of the ship, making it inoperable.

We learnt that we captured 24 merchant vessels and they were being moved to a special naval anchorage off Paradip Port for search for contraband, after which they would either be released or apprehended.

10 December 1971

There was insufficient wind on deck. A planned Sea Hawk launch had to be cancelled. One Alizé aircraft was launched at 1.20 a.m. to destroy the ordnance factory near Chittagong; it carried out a successful bombing of the factory. Two Alizés were launched at 11.00 a.m. They bombed the airfield at Cox's Bazar, putting it out of action completely.

Information had been received that one of the three Alizé aircraft that were operating on the west coast from Bombay under the command of Lt Cdr Ashok Roy was shot down somewhere in the Arabian Sea while investigating a high-frequency bearing. Crew members Lt Cdr Ashok Roy, Lt H.S. Sirohi and M.K. Vijayan were on the missing list.

11 December 1971

An Alizé aircraft was launched to bomb Chiringa airstrip. This was probably an abandoned airfield, but it was bombed and put out of use. Another Alizé, IN 201, was launched to carry out a recce from Pusur River towards the east, along the coast up to Hatia Island and Meghna River, in order to locate a boat reported to be carrying the chief of the Pakistan naval force. A camouflaged tug of the Pakistan Navy towing two other crafts was sighted; on reaching closer, it was revealed that the tug had a gun boat tied up alongside.

The Alizé attacked the tug and gun boat with rockets and depth charges. The two craft being towed detached themselves, and the tug and the gun boat were sunk. When the Alizé was attacking the gun boat, it was hit by gunfire and sustained seven bullet hits. The main and emergency inverters, compass, fuel flow meter, radar, artificial horizon and other vital instruments, including the radio transmission and intercom system, packed up due to the bullet hits. To add to these difficulties, there was hydraulic failure and, therefore, bomb bays could not be closed. All services were lowered on emergency system and, at 110 knots, the aircraft headed for the *Vikrant*, the mother ship. In order to reduce the extra weight, a few sonobuoys were jettisoned. The crew displayed great courage and presence of mind in dealing with the emergency and returned to the ship safely.

Another report was received around 4.40 p.m., which said that the officers of the Pakistani forces were leaving East Pakistan by small boats. One Alizé aircraft was kept airborne throughout the night for surveillance and recce of the area. The first Alizé aircraft reported four radar contacts. The information was passed on to INS *Beas* and INS *Brahmaputra*, who sank them immediately.

12 December 1971

The wind was blowing since morning and picking up speed. Four Sea Hawks were launched with two bombs each to attack the Chittagong runway. Six out of eight bombs fell on the runway and made big craters on the surface. The next sorties carried out rocket attacks on ships. One ship was set on fire and two ships were heavily damaged. The aircraft continued their attacks throughout the day. The runway surface of Chittagong airport was severely damaged, rendering it unusable by aircraft to take-off or land. All spotted ships were sunk or destroyed and warehouses went up in flames. Two anti-aircraft gun batteries were put out of action and silenced.

The squadron of Sea Hawks flew 29 sorties and dropped a total of 40 bombs. Around 30 found their targets, which was a creditable record. The anti-aircraft fire from the enemy ground batteries was heavy but did not seem to bother our aircrew. Each of the squadron pilots struck the enemy targets with determination and complete disregard for anti-aircraft ground fire.

Lt Prem Kumar's and Lt Dutta's front windscreens were shattered by gunfire when they dived to attack the enemy gun positions. It was to their credit that they kept their nerve even after their view from the cockpit was badly affected. They displayed exceptional flying skills and brought their aircraft back to the ship safely.

The *Vikrant* was requested to provide air support to the army. The Sea Hawks launched from the *Vikrant* could not establish contact with the army units on the ground. They did not see any troops in the thick hilly jungles and had to return to the ship. Chittagong city was under a pall of thick black smoke rising from the warehouses and ships attacked by the Sea Hawks.

After the recovery of the last aircraft, the Captain expressed his appreciation for the determined attacks by the squadron in the face of heavy enemy gunfire.

13 December 1971

It was another day of continuous flying. The squadron launched Sea Hawks in waves throughout the day. The squadron once again emerged with flying colours. Twenty-two sorties were carried out with mixed armament. The aircraft attacked four ships up a river, the secondary runway, ordnance factory, anti-aircraft batteries and Pakistan Armed Constabulary area. All ships in the area were either on fire or had run aground. A tanker blew up when hit by a 500-pound bomb from a Sea Hawk. The Sea Hawks bombed the area and carried out the strikes, exercising care and caution for life and property of the civilian population. There was information that Pakistani troops may attempt to fly out to Burma. The Sea Hawks were scheduled to attack the cantonment the next day and level it to the ground.

The Flag Officer Commanding Eastern Fleet, Rear Admiral S.H. Sarma, was immensely pleased with the ship and the squadrons. Vice Admiral N. Krishnan had sent an encouraging signal to the Sea Hawk squadron. Our squadron surpassed everyone's expectations. The aircraft serviceability and availability was incredible and impressive, even to us. Ever since the war began, the squadron never had to cancel any planned sortie or launch from the ship for want of aircraft.

All doubts about the operational and strategic worth of a carrier-based naval aviation to assist the surface navy in exercising area control at sea, as well as denial of passage to our adversaries, were put to rest. The performance of the *Vikrant* and her squadrons in this war made acquisition of new aircraft to replace ageing Sea Hawks a certainty, and acquisition of one or two new carriers a distinct need for the country.

14 December 1971

The first phase of the war was nearing its end. The landing of 1,500 troops by our ships *Magar*, *Guldar* and *Gharial* was delayed by 24 hours. It was scheduled to take place the next day. The idea was for these troops to land near Cox's Bazar and cut off any escape attempt for the Pakistanis into Myanmar. The original idea was for the *Vikrant* to provide air support to our soldiers. It was not possible to do so now. The *Vikrant* was running low on fuel, rations and stores. The fuel in the ship was down to 25 per cent. Food and essentials needed replenishment. The *Vikrant* was ordered to proceed to Paradip.

The *Vikrant* continued to fly her aircraft. Our squadron's work consisted of launching four Sea Hawks to carry out rocket attack on the Army barracks in the cantonment area. The photographs taken by the aircraft during the attack showed that the weapons found their targets. The aircrew and maintenance personnel had a well-earned rest for the next two days. The ship and the squadron returned to the war zone. The AEO used the break to carry out essential maintenance work on the aircraft. He also focussed on repairing the aircraft damaged by enemy gunfire.

There was news regarding the movement of a task group of the American Seventh Fleet into our area with the US aircraft carrier, *Enterprise*. It was perceived as an attempt by the Americans to frighten India and influence the outcome of the war. The Americans were to soon learn that India and her armed forces meant business and there was not much they could do to help Pakistan.

The year 1971 will be remembered as the 'Year of India' for a long time.

≈

PART THREE

10

Surrender and Thereafter

From 13 December 1971, there were signs from the Pakistani camp in East Pakistan that they were losing their nerve. The Pakistani forces in East Pakistan were caught between the Indian Army and the IAF attacks from the north, a total sea and air blockade, and attacks from the naval fighter jets of INS *Vikrant* from the south in the Bay of Bengal. The Pakistanis had no hope of getting any help from West Pakistan, nor was there any way to escape from East Pakistan. The Indian Navy had blockaded and sealed the sea and skies in both the Arabian Sea and the Bay of Bengal.

Victory: Pakistan Collapses

The Sea Hawk jet fighters launched from INS *Vikrant* were attacking vital installations and military targets in East Pakistan, putting them out of action and sinking ships and craft in ports and rivers. Pakistan was staring down the barrel with total collapse of its fighting ability and morale in the west as well as in the east. With certain and inevitable annihilation by the Indian forces staring the Pakistanis in the face, Governor Abdul Motaleb Malik of East Pakistan called a meeting of the high officials at the Government House in Dacca, on 14 December, to take stock of the situation, which was worsening by the hour and rapidly slipping out of hand. An IAF fighter jet aircraft mounted an attack and strafed the Government House just when the meeting was in progress. Governor Malik lost his nerve and resigned immediately.

Lt Gen. Niazi received a signal from the President of Pakistan, Yahya Khan, on 14 December at noon time:

> You have now reached a stage where further resistance is no longer humanly possible nor will it serve any useful purpose. It will only lead to further loss of life and destruction. You should now take all necessary measures to stop the fighting and preserve the lives of all armed force personnel, all those from West Pakistan and all loyal elements....[1]

Meanwhile, the IAF stepped up attacks and bombed the command-post of Lt Gen. Niazi in Dacca cantonment. He finally decided to lay down arms and surrender to the Indian armed forces; he conveyed this to Gen. Manekshaw through the US embassy, and the message was received at 2.30 p.m. on 15 December. The Instrument of Surrender was accepted and initialled at 2.45 p.m. on 16 December. It was decided that the armed forces of East Pakistan would surrender formally at a ceremony to be held at Dacca the same afternoon.

The Ramna Race Course ground, also called the Paltan Maidan, in Dacca, the capital of East Pakistan, was the venue selected for the surrender ceremony. A group of helicopters flying in formation landed at the Tezgaon airfield in the afternoon of 16 December. They carried Lt Gen. Jagjit Singh Aurora, GOC-in-C Eastern Command; accompanied by Air Marshal H.C. Dewan, air officer commanding-in-chief Eastern Air Command; Vice

---

[1]Prasad, S.N., and U.P. Thapliyal (eds), *The India Pakistan War of 1971: A History*, Natraj Publishers, 2019, p. 410.

Admiral N. Krishnan, flag officer commanding-in-chief, Eastern Naval Command; Lt Gen. Sagat Singh, general officer commanding 4 Corps; and all his divisional commanders; Group Captain Khondekar, chief of staff of the Mukti Bahini; representative of the provisional government of Bangladesh; Ashok Ray of the Indian Ministry of External Affairs; and a number of press representatives for the surrender ceremony.

The Instrument of Surrender was signed by Lt Gen. Niazi and Lt Gen. Aurora in the presence of a large crowd of Bangladeshis, and journalists and reporters representing the Indian and the international media. Lt Gen. Niazi removed his lanyard and handed it over. He also handed over his pistol to Lt Gen. Aurora as a token of surrender. Indira Gandhi, the PM of India, informed the Lok Sabha at 5.30 p.m. on 16 December about the surrender of the West Pakistani forces in Bangladesh. She announced, 'Dacca is now the free capital of a free country.'[2]

The setting winter sun over the Ramna Race Course signalled the end of the 24 years of Pakistan's rule over East Pakistan, which was now a new independent country, Bangladesh. India thus fulfilled the commitment it had made to the people of Bangladesh.

Fallout

The achievements of the Indian Navy during the war are commendable. Ships and aircraft of the Indian Navy sank one Pakistani destroyer, *Khaibar*, one minesweeper, *Muhafiz*, one submarine Ghazi, three patrol craft *Jessore*, *Comilla* and *Sylhet*, 14 converted gunboats and damaged one tanker, *Dacca*. It is estimated that along with these surface vessels and a submarine, the Pakistan Navy lost about 55 officers and 430 sailors. The Indian

---

[2]'Statements by Mrs. Gandhi on Truce and Surrender', *The New York Times*, 17 December 1971, https://tinyurl.com/2avwea5k. Accessed on 18 August 2023.

Navy lost one frigate, *Khukri*, and one Alizé aircraft, besides 20 officers and 180 sailors.[3]

The total damage in the east was formidable: 13 merchant ships with a total tonnage of about 94,000 tons were sunk by the attacks of the Indian Navy jet fighters that took off from INS *Vikrant* during the war. These included five Pakistani ships—*Surma* of 5,890 tons, *Anis Baksh* of 6,273 tons, *Karnaphuli* of 9,123 tons, *Al Abbas* of 8,559 tons and *Rangamati* of 8,909 tons; one Danish ship *African Proctor*, four Greek ships—*Thetis* of 2,276 tons, *Mastro Stelios* of 8,823 tons, *Avlos* of 11,237 tons and *Chrysovalandou* of 8,151 tons—one Swedish ship *Star Altair* of 8,962 tons, one Spanish ship *Ondarda* of 8,259 tons and one Somalian ship *Lightning* of 7,046 tons. Eight merchant ships belonging to Pakistan, Denmark, Liberia and New Zealand were damaged. Besides these, 36 small craft (35 Pakistani and one Dutch) were sunk and 18 damaged in East Pakistan.[4]

This short war of a fortnight brought about significant results in the total collapse of Pakistan. The speed and extent of its collapse surprised even the international observers and friends of Pakistan. Pakistan suffered a quick resounding collapse and a humiliating defeat. As many as 93,000 of Pakistan's uniformed armed forces' officers and men, including its seniormost general in East Pakistan, admitted defeat, laid down arms and surrendered in Dacca to the Indian forces led by Lt Gen. Aurora. The creation of Bangladesh altered the geopolitical scene of the region permanently to India's advantage. India and the Indian armed forces rose in stature worldwide for their military resolve and discipline displayed during the war, and then in providing humane treatment to the defeated armed force personnel of Pakistan. All this impressed the international community.

---

[3]Prasad, S.N., and U.P. Thapliyal (eds), *The India Pakistan War of 1971: A History*, Natraj Publishers, 2019, p. 484–85.
[4]Ibid. 482.

Pakistan, an avowed adversary of India ever since its creation in 1947, was humbled and weakened. What remained of Pakistan was a truncated, demoralized country, a shadow of its former self. With Pakistan removed permanently from the Bay of Bengal, India's control and influence over the seas in the region improved with easier and freer access to the Far East through the Strait of Malacca. It also brought a renewed focus on the need to improve maritime influence and sea control of the Bay of Bengal by improving the Indian naval presence in the Indian territories of Andaman and Nicobar Islands, an archipelago consisting of 571 big and small islands situated at a distance of 800 nautical miles from the eastern coastline of mainland India. India's decision to set up a national tri-service, Joint Strategic Forces Command, in Andaman and Nicobar Islands, and upgradation of the force levels in the Islands can be viewed as an outcome of the churn in the Indian national security policy after the 1971 war. It remains an ongoing process.

The friendly and amicable relations of India and Bangladesh since 1971 have also opened up prospects of trade, commerce, communication and cultural relations with nations further to the east of India. In fact, an 'Act East' policy is now the cornerstone of Indian foreign policy. Not that such a policy had not been thought of earlier, but it took a renewed vigour, dynamism and a firmer shape only after the 1971 war. The northeastern states of India have gained importance and there is a focussed awareness among the Indian planners to pay greater attention to this region in terms of all fields of development, like better communication, improved roads and access to the region.

New sea routes and land routes by road and rail between India and Bangladesh have opened, and more have been planned for the mutual benefit of the two nations. The process is ongoing and is leading to greater harmony and prosperity on both sides. With improved understanding and mutual goodwill, the land borders between India and Bangladesh have been rationalized with mutual negotiations and agreement, resulting in a streamlined relationship and greater volume of trade between the two nations. There is also the promising prospect of further sharing of the river waters, development of road, rail and sea routes, and exploitation of the natural resources between India and Bangladesh to mutual advantage and benefit.

Looking Back

The 1971 war happened 24 years after India's independence. India discovered for the first time its latent strength, because it had never tested it in full measure and was, therefore, unaware of it. The true potential of the Indian armed forces lay in their working together in a cohesive and integrated manner, each controlling its area of strength; the Indian Army on land, IAF in air and the Indian Navy at sea.

With the navy performing and executing its classic naval combat role to control and dominate the Arabian Sea in the west and Bay of Bengal in the east, the army and air force could unleash their fire power on the adversary from land and air, while the navy held the adversary tightly in a naval blockade. Naval combative action in the form of missile attacks destroyed the warships of the Pakistani naval fleet in Karachi and caused widespread devastation and destruction to the defence infrastructure of Pakistan. It also gave a body blow to the economy of Pakistan and triggered its economic collapse, since Karachi was also the country's commercial capital. Simultaneously, the carrier battle group of the Indian Navy, operating in the Bay of Bengal on the eastern seaboard, struck heavy blows on ships, ports and cities of East Pakistan. As the Indian Navy had blocked the SLOC in the Arabian Sea and in the Bay of Bengal, the sea communications and exchange of goods and people between East and West Pakistan were cut off. No help or assistance could reach Pakistan—neither from the east nor from the west—and the demoralized Pakistanis could not escape to safety because a naval blockade had sealed all entry and exit routes by sea. In the Bay of Bengal, the jet fighters of INS *Vikrant* controlled the sea and the airspace, both of which were denied to the adversary.

India discovered that when the navy unleashed its full potential, the country's strength multiplied to achieve the national objectives. Both India and the Indian Navy learnt their lessons well, and the period post-1971 has seen the Indian Navy grow from strength to strength. Since then, India has given the much needed priority in allocation of funds and resources for the development of the navy. Indian Navy's self-esteem, confidence and its stature in the public perception have grown manifold.

India also learnt the benefits of thorough planning before going in for an offensive action against an adversary. The decision to delay action against Pakistan from mid-1971 to December 1971 gave ample time for the three armed forces to prepare for the oncoming situation and integrate with each other to define and understand the role of each force. It also took advantage of the weather conditions by avoiding action in the monsoon months of July–September. The decision to launch the operations in 1971-end provided the crucial five to six months to the Indian Navy to plan, practise and perfect the deployment of the missile boats for attack on Karachi. This proved crucial as subsequent events showed.

The war also demonstrated how by denying the use of sea to an adversary, the enemy could be starved of vital supplies by laying a sea blockade to close the enemy's SLOC. It was a welcome revelation and learning experience for the Indian Navy and for the nation.

Admiral S.M. Nanda, as the CNS from March 1970 to February 1973, was single-handedly responsible for introducing the new thinking at the naval headquarters. He was the author of the new, strategically offensive approach pursued by the Indian Navy in the 1971 Indo-Pak War in the Arabian Sea as well as in the Bay of Bengal. His contribution in providing an efficient and strong leadership as well as direction to the Indian Navy with an all-out, no holds barred naval attacks on Karachi and East Pakistan paid immediate dividends.

Admiral Nanda wrote in his memoirs:

…before the 1971 war, there were very few who appreciated the role of the Indian Navy and what it could do to safeguard national security. Such a state of affairs had made me more determined to demonstrate, should the occasion present itself, that the Navy could and would play a positive role instead of merely being a passive and defensive arm, as had been its role in earlier wars. I had made up my mind to do so and began meticulously evolving the strategy of positive offensive action… The underlying principle on both eastern and western seaboards was positive action. The Indian Navy's bold action proved to the nation and the people its usefulness in safeguarding India's national interests. Its role and capabilities have never been questioned thereafter. I can clearly recall to this day that up to that time hardly anybody took the Navy seriously.

The greatest achievement of the 1971 war was that the government understood its role, i.e., of denying the enemy use of the sea supply routes whilst giving our own logistic suppliers complete freedom; and of having a moving airfield with powerful strike aircraft that could wreak havoc on an unsuspecting enemy. The question of the Navy being irrelevant or redundant in the national security matrix never arose again… It was for the first time that the Indian Navy had done something visible and dramatic that provided a great sense of satisfaction to the rest of the country. Till then, our people had been accustomed to look to our land borders for news from the war front.

The Naval operations in this war suddenly presented a new front to the people of India, and the news from this front— both from the Bay of Bengal and the Arabian Sea—was exciting and encouraging. They appreciated what they read in the newspapers or heard on the radio about significant events such as our raid on Karachi, the sinking of the Pak submarine Ghazi and our total control of the Bay of Bengal. The Indian Navy was able to stop supplies from reaching the beleaguered Pak Army and prevented them from escaping by sea. The achievements of the country's smallest and youngest service, the Indian Navy, comforted people greatly.[5]

After the 1971 war, India and the Indians had, for the first time in Indian history, a clear vision of the role of the Indian Navy in the security matrix of the nation keeping pace with the modern times, and the changing centre of gravity of the geopolitical situation in the Pacific and Indian Oceans. The Indian Navy has assumed a demonstrable three-dimensional capability of operating at high seas—warships on surface, nuclear and conventional submarines under the sea; state-of-the-art aircraft carrier-borne jet fighters; long-range maritime reconnaissance aircraft and mid-air refuelling. The navy also integrated with the Strategic Forces Command created in 2003. The navies of the developed nations attach importance to participating in periodic exercises with the three-dimensional Indian Navy. The naval cooperation of the Quad nations—the US, Japan, Australia and India—is the proof of the growing importance of the Indian Navy among the navies of the developed world.

As for the *Vikrant*, even though Pakistan surrendered to the Indian armed forces on 16 December, she continued to patrol the

[5]Nanda, S.M., *The Man Who Bombed Karachi: A Memoir*, HarperCollins Publishers India, 2004, p. 250.

northern waters of the Bay of Bengal to monitor the situation till calm and normalcy prevailed.

In the following decade, the *Vikrant* became the subject of a roaring debate between two opposing schools of thought that concerned themselves with the Indian Navy: one favouring aircraft carrier-based Navy, following the example of the US, and the other wanting an emphasis on the submarines instead, a concept practised by the USSR. India has not made a choice yet and the country continues to strengthen the navy in all the three dimensions: surface, carrier-based naval aviation and the submarines.

The factors that determine a nation's supremacy over the seas are well known. It is their adoption and timely implementation that are problematic, because of the resources required. Britain rose in the eighteenth century to become a colonial power in Asia and Africa due to its strong navy that had been evolving from the sixteenth century; it had an experience of over 200 years of operating far and wide in the oceans and seas. Apart from protecting the military interests of Britain, it ensured unhindered trade traffic by the British maritime ships around the globe. A country is a sea power if it has a strong navy for sea control and a large commercial fleet to serve its maritime trade interests. It has been said that any land-based army would submit to a strong naval blockade. This proposition was proved right by the Indian Navy's blockade of East Pakistan and West Pakistan in the 1971 Indo-Pak War. It took just two weeks of blockading of the Bay of Bengal for the Pakistani armed forces to collapse, give in, lay down their arms and surrender.

Developing countries like India have to defend their home waters and retain the capacity to operate at distant seas simultaneously. In many cases, the naval forces of a country are not large enough to do both. Some argue that deployment of big ships in home waters and sufficient naval strength in distant seas would be a good proposition. Others favour submarines to defend the home waters and capital ships to safeguard national interests at distant places. The solution probably lies in between, but each nation has to work out the conundrum and find a practical solution for itself.

THE PICKLED WAR

This incident is narrated by Commodore Gurnam Singh from his personal experience from the war.

The turbulent Bay of Bengal was the eastern theatre of the war of 1971, where the Indian Navy flotilla had laid siege, blocking all sea lanes to and from the then East Pakistan. INS *Vikrant* was the flagship spearheading the formidable naval force with a number of destroyers, frigates, submarines and other ships and craft under the command of this carrier battle group. The *Vikrant* was operating with her full complement of two frontline aircraft squadrons—the White Tigers operating the Sea Hawk fighter jet aircraft and the King Cobras operating the anti-submarine Alizé turboprop aircraft. These aircraft were in complete control of the skies over the Bay of Bengal and kept a sharp eye on the waters below for any vessel trying to sneak through the naval blockade that was in force.

I was then a lieutenant serving on board INS *Vikrant* as the AEO of the White Tigers squadron. For us in the squadron, time had ceased to exist. The aircraft serviceability was all that mattered. When the aircraft were serviceable, and fit to fly, they would be sent to the flight deck to join the operations. Those aircraft that needed maintenance, servicing or defect rectification were worked upon non-stop in the aircraft hangars below the flight deck till they became serviceable and were ready to join other fly-worthy aircraft on the flight deck. The cycle went on and on, just as we had trained ourselves during the flying exercises for months before the hostilities broke out on 3 December. The system worked like a well-oiled machine.

The officers' mess of INS *Vikrant*, called 'wardroom' in naval parlance, was where all officers took their breakfast, lunch and dinner. We had been in the operational area for months now, sailing up and down the length and breadth of the Bay of Bengal—patrolling, exercising, playing war games with other ships and craft of the fleet, carrying out night exercises and keeping a hawk's eye on the vast expanses of the waters of the Bay of Bengal to ensure it was closed to foes and secured for the impending operations.

INS *Vikrant* was like a small township. One needed to move between the hangars, flight deck, lower decks, workshops, libraries, stores, machinery spaces, canteens, administrative offices and many other facilities on different decks of the ship—it provided enough exercise. It kept everyone physically fit and worked up sharp appetites.

Everyone looked forward to the meal hour. The mess staff prepared a daily menu of delicious dishes showcasing the best of their skills. Some of us, however, had minor food addictions. We would always request some extra green chillies, onions, fresh lemons, and mango or lemon pickle as accompaniment to the meal. These were minor indulgences but added something infinitely special to the meal; the mess staff would willingly oblige, as such requests were anticipated and adequately catered for. Meanwhile, the war went on.

A few weeks later, we faced a small problem. The fresh provisions stocked by the ship prior to the commencement of the operations were beginning to run out. The mess shifted to tinned rations, like tinned biryani, tinned rice, tinned meat, tinned fruits, etc. They were pleasing to the palate initially, but as the days went by, there was a longing for fresh vegetables. Gradually, the supply of pickles, chillies and lemons too dwindled, and the mess staff informed us with embarrassment that these items were now out of stock. There was a noticeable decline in the amount of food eaten and the appetite of the officers. The mess staff tried out different tricks of their trade but to no avail. There was little they, or for that matter anyone else, could do. Pickles, onions, chillies, lemons and other condiments were not critical to the operations, but they were missed badly in the mess. Food was no longer relished.

Then came the news of Pakistan's surrender. The war had ended. The guns fell silent. The news bulletins broadcast by the ship were eagerly awaited and lapped up for details. East Pakistan had now become an independent new nation called Bangladesh. The war that had permeated our beings slowly began to leave us and we began to live normal lives once again. People began to remember their families, and writing letters once again became the favourite pastime.

Two or three days later, we learnt that one of our ship's helicopters was going to Chittagong, one of the main cities of the new country, which our aircraft had pounded for the previous two weeks. A special request was conveyed through proper channels for some pickles and other fresh vegetables to be purchased from the shore. The 'angels of mercy', as the helicopters are called on board the ships because of their SAR mission capability at sea, returned after a couple of hours with two 15-kg tins of Chittagong special pickle, and two gunny bags full of other fresh provisions.

The news of the special consignment from Chittagong somehow leaked and spread by word of mouth. That day, the mess staff prepared a special dinner and served it with a green salad consisting of fresh green chillies and lemons, with pride of place reserved for the just imported pickle. It brought a special cheer to the wardroom and our appetites returned with full vigour. It is possible that those two tins of mango pickle were among the first items exported by the just-born Bangladesh to India. Our immediate thoughts, however, were with the more mundane things—the hot meal and the parathas to be relished with the Chittagong pickle. The combination was heavenly.

11

The Legacy

The 1971 war has left a lasting legacy. The most important one is, of course, the nation of Bangladesh, which still thrives and has maintained cordial relations with India. The other important legacy of the war is the realization of the importance of the navy for Indian defences. The Indian Navy is now a developed force with all the support of the government. It has grown in might and can stand on its own on the world stage. This would never have happened without the success of 1971 and the evident powerful role the Indian Navy played in Pakistan's defeat.

Today, 75 years later, the Indian Navy is counted seventh in world ranking[1], after the US, China, Russia, Indonesia, Korea and Japan.

The Indian Navy plans to have three aircraft carriers on the inventory[2], which will allow it to operate two carrier task forces or battle groups at all times with 150 jet-fighter aircraft. As for

---

[1]'Global Naval Powers Ranking (2023)', *WDMMW*, https://tinyurl.com/3hjnwsjv. Accessed on 23 August 2023.

[2]'Prepping For Another India-Made Aircraft Carrier: Navy's Big Announcement', *NDTV*, 1 September 2023, https://tinyurl.com/yn8x4kp8. Accessed on 5 September 2023.

the manpower, the navy has about 70,000 officers and sailors. It is clearly seen that the size and the capability of the navy of free India, inherited from the outgoing British in 1947, was a tiny fraction of the size of the navy the country needed.

What If?

The role of the valiant organs of the naval aviation of 1971 would be better understood if the readers did a 'what if' exercise:

What if the *Vikrant* had not been seaworthy in 1971? Without the *Vikrant*, what shape and form would the naval operations have taken in the Bay of Bengal against East Pakistan? India would have won the 1971 war, but it may not have been the thumping victory won with blockading the Bay of Bengal and attacking of East Pakistan by the fighter jets of INS *Vikrant*. The marine engineers did a marvellous job in making the *Vikrant* operational for flying her squadrons despite the less-than-optimum condition of the ship's boilers.

What if the *Vikrant* had been seaworthy but the Indian Navy did not have enough Sea Hawks to make a viable Sea Hawk jet-fighter squadron in 'fighter ground attack' role to operate from the carrier? Without an operational jet-fighter squadron with 18 aircraft, would the *Vikrant* have been committed to war? Highly improbable!

What if the Indian Navy had not purchased the 28 old Sea Hawks from Germany in 1966–67 after Germany stopped flying them? Would we have been able to muster enough fighter aircraft for the frontline unit establishment of INAS 300 for embarked operations for war? By October 1971, just before going to war, the Indian Navy was left with just 33 Sea Hawks from the 74 purchased, the rest having been lost to attrition. The 18 Sea Hawks that went to war had 13 German Sea Hawks among them. It is not commonly known that the German Sea Hawks deal of 1966–67 played a crucial and critical role in the 1971 Indo-Pak War. Without this deal, the scenario in 1971 of the carrier-borne fighter operations would have been very different. INAS 300 would not have had viable number of Sea Hawks to operate from INS *Vikrant* and go to war.

Lest We Forget

In the 1960s, our naval aviation was modelled on the infrastructure existing in the British Royal Navy for their naval aircraft, albeit modified and scaled down to match the Indian Navy's needs, and tailored to the limited resources of the nation. The organizations in the naval aviation branch of the Indian Navy, and the officers and men working in them, made a stellar contribution towards ensuring an all-embracing growth in every sector of the Indian naval aviation in the 15 years from 1956–1971. It was their contribution that made it possible for the Indian Navy to exploit the old warships and jet fighter aircraft, much beyond the age at which all other foreign nations had scrapped them and withdrawn them from active frontline service. Theirs is a silent, unsung contribution that has so far gone unnoticed and unacknowledged, except by way of a passing mention by some of the authors who have written about the Indian Navy and Indian naval aviation.

It is the recommendation of the authors that the role of INS *Vikrant* and the naval aviation squadrons be recognized and saluted in a befitting manner to show our collective recognition of their excellent performance. In this aspect, the Indian Navy could do well to follow the traditions of the Indian Army of bestowing battle honours on the units that take part in operations and display exceptional courage and bravery. INS *Vikrant*, INAS 300 Sea Hawk squadron, INAS 310 Alizé anti-submarine squadron and INAS 321 Chetak helicopters SAR squadron played stellar roles in preparing for and in the conduct of the 1971 Indo-Pak

War. These four units ought to be honoured for their contribution in the war and awarded on the lines of the Indian Army units, which are awarded in their own right, in addition to the awards and medals conferred on the individuals for valour, bravery, courage and devotion displayed during the operations.

Navy Day is celebrated on 4 December. The Indian Navy celebrated 2021–22 as the golden jubilee year of India's victory in the 1971 Indo-Pak War. Post celebration, it is a fit occasion for our nation to consider conferring the units with battle honours for their singularly salutary performance in the Bangladesh Liberation War.

The *Vikrant*, most affectionately remembered by those who sailed in her, is no more, but the award should be bestowed on her posthumously and should be received and held by India's new aircraft carrier which, it has been decided, will carry the old *Vikrant*'s legacy and her name.

The same logic applies to the Sea Hawk squadron. Sea Hawks have flown into the sunset, but the old INAS 300 lives on as a legend and an icon. This squadron should be conferred with battle honours, and these should be received by the new INAS 300. As for the successors and inheritors of the legendry INAS 310, which does not operate Alizés anymore (they retired in late '90s), their honours should be received and held by the Indian Navy's current anti-submarine aircraft squadron. The SAR helicopters squadron operating from the new *Vikrant* should receive the honours on behalf of the INAS 321.

In honouring these four iconic units, our nation and the Indian Navy would indeed honour themselves and also establish a new tradition. It will also keep the names and achievements of the old *Vikrant* and her three squadrons, which went to war, alive, and inspire and ignite patriotic fervour in the present and future generations.

Afterword
We Put the Screws On

Vice Admiral S.K.K. Krishnan (Retd)

The motto of the NBCD School—'To float, to move, to fight'—comes to mind when I think of the role played by the Engine Room department of the *Vikrant* during the 1971 operations. The performance of the Engine Room team was legendary. They managed an impaired propulsion system so well that flying operations of the ship continued without a glitch and our naval aviation wing excelled at the war front.

In March 1971, when the East Pakistan issue started emerging, the *Vikrant* was literally a sitting duck in Bombay, with one boiler cracked and all other boilers clearly indicating sub-surface cracks. One couldn't believe when a senior sailor doing his evening rounds located seepage of water from one of the water drums of the A1 boiler. More detailed examination revealed that the drum had a crack along its riveted joint. In those days, the navy did not have the facility to radiograph such thicknesses of steel, and Bhabha Atomic Research Centre had to be roped in. They examined all four boilers and sent their results on strips of films. I, as a sub-lieutenant at the time, was made to sit in the hallowed corner office of the then Chief Staff Officer (Technical) to convert them into pencil sketches, so that the severity of the problem could be understood by all. Although only the A1 boiler water drum had displayed slow seepage of water, all other drums had a few sub-surface cracks, which could propagate anytime.

The discovery of the insipient crack gave rise to a serious concern for the safety of the boiler and the ship when steaming. The immediate expert opinion was to declare her unfit to sail and fly her aircraft. The *Vikrant* was the flagship of the Indian naval fleet and the pride of the Indian Navy. The prognosis had a profound depressing effect on her and the fleet. When Capt. Kirpal Singh left in early 1971 after completing his tenure, no new captain was appointed. The ship was tied up at Ballard Pier Extension for nearly three months, as no one seemed to know what would happen. The first sign of life came when the ship was 'cold moved' to anchorage to avoid any damage to the hull during the onset of monsoon. An acting captain was appointed, as all the other senior captains sought more dashing appointments to command other frontline ships. Once we were at anchorage, we could sense a wind of change. After being at anchor for 100 days, the ship was dry-docked for some essential repairs, and within two weeks of undocking, we set sail to the east coast. Capt. Swaraj Parkash took over command.

Before we left, we were told in no uncertain terms what was in store for us at the other end. I vividly remember the thundering speech made by Rear Admiral (later vice admiral) E.C. Kuruvilla, the fleet commander, and another one by Babu Jagjivan Ram, our defence minister. We knew we were heading in harm's way. However, most of the crew on board, especially those involved with flying aircraft off the deck, were unsure how we would ever be able to operate with such a doubtful propulsion system.

Only three boilers were available and the A1 Boiler, which was critical for charging steam to the catapult, was out of action. After months of lying idle, all other machineries were also suspect, and even a simple snag could make flying operations risky. Moreover, the east coast had no shore support to offer, with only a small engineering workshop available at Madras. We, in the Engine Room department, put up a bold front and carried on as if everything would be fine. We went ahead with our jobs with undisguised bravado, and fortune, as usual, favoured the brave. The Commander (E) had only one thing to say to all his officers when he called us for a pep talk: 'If I am ever to be seen in a boiler suit, shame on you all.' That was like a whiplash and we knew our prestige was at stake.

Our defence against possible boiler burst were elementary methods, such as placing a protective steel band around the riveted joints of the boiler drums or reducing the boiler pressure by a few PSI (pounds per sq. inch). At best, they were psychological buttresses against a possible disaster. These steps might sound rudimentary, but the drills we went through were not. Boiler emergencies were practised to perfection and so were other contingencies. An extra watch keeper was posted near the boiler gauge glass, to keep a close watch of level fluctuations, especially during catapult charging. The main steam range was cross connected between both engine rooms, so that the only boiler in the forward engine room was supported adequately, especially when the catapult was charged. All junior engineer officers had to go through a drill of getting completely blindfolded while sitting in the ward room in 4R compartment and walk up to 4M compartment to start the M7 diesel generator. We had to not only walk up to there but also locate the starting air valve, start the diesel generator and quickly open the cooling water line, all while being blindfolded.

Even before we left the harbour, we had a serious problem. We couldn't make feedwater with our evaporators. The water in Bombay harbour was dirty due to monsoon turbulence and we had just enough feedwater to last about three watches (12 hours). However, we set sail as scheduled and kept struggling with the five evaporators as we left the harbour. Finally, before we reached Goa, we started making more feedwater than what we consumed.

Just as we reached Madras, one of the extraction pumps had a bearing failure. Many officers in the wardroom had that 'I told you so' look on their faces. Suddenly, everyone seemed to know the role of the extraction pump and how the ship could not move relying on just one motor-driven extraction pump. Well, they had miscalculated the resolve of the Engine Room department. Within a couple of days, we were back in business, with the extraction pump humming as ever. Thereafter, the ship ran like a proverbial sewing machine. Spirits were high and no one realized we were sailing on three suspicious boilers. There were many occasions when major jobs, normally undertaken by the dockyard, were completed by the ship staff, using the limited workshop facility on board. Problems were plenty, but the never-say-die attitude helped resolve them with ease.

The first few launches of aircraft were nail biting. Over time, the drill of charging the catapult somewhat slowly (to reduce pressure variations of the boilers) and building up the ship's speed delicately to achieve the 'wind on deck condition' was perfected. As the entire ship gained confidence, everyone and everything fell in place, and flying operations were conducted with relative ease. Surely, it was not the same as in its heyday, but it was far better than what the doomsday predictors had anticipated.

Engineers grew in esteem and were given some minor privileges. Cabins with portholes, like 4R 103 and 4R 109, were allocated to Engineering Branch officers. Occasionally, while coming off watch from the hot engine rooms, we were even allowed to grab a beer from the rear door of the anteroom bar. The Engine Room department became frontrunners in many activities. There was nothing that we could not do. We were completely charged up and willing to take calculated risks, and the spirit of the department was unmatchable. We won most of the interdepartmental competitions, including a famous football match, which was decided on a penalty shootout. The departmental concert team was the most popular, with Patil, leading mechanic (engineering) of the flight deck section belting out Kishore Kumar songs with ease. Senior Engineer Lt Cdr Bhushan kept the ward room enthralled with his jokes of Bakshi Ghulam Mohammad. The camaraderie in the ward room was superb.

Amongst all the busy and nerve-wracking activities, there were many fun moments too. Since we left Bombay in a hurry, the welfare officer had not found time to pick up any 16-mm movies from the film library in Angre. So, we were left with just two Hindi movies, *Caravan* and *Mera Sayaa*. The usual drill was to screen a movie on the flight deck in the evening after flying operations and screen it again in the afternoon in the ward room for officers. That drill continued and all of us saw these two movies time and again. Most of us knew the dialogues by heart. 'Monica, Oh My Darling' from *Caravan* and 'Aur Phir Kya Hua' from *Mera Saaya* were adapted suitably during ward room banter.

CNS Admiral Nanda visited the ship to see for himself how well the ship had worked up the squadrons. A shop window was scheduled, and the first hawk was on the chocks. Suddenly, there was a hush on the deck. The catapult light that shows it is serviceable to launch aircraft was off. That's when the FDEO's expertise came out on public display. His sixth sense told him why one particular lamp did not light up in the howdah panel[1]. Lt Cdr Suresh Soota, the FDEO, the officer who operated the catapult to launch the aircraft, ran from his place near the howdah to the fore end of the catapult, opened up a flap and cleaned the lens with his handkerchief near the 'snail's eye' lamp. Before the *Vikrant* captain and Admiral Nanda, standing on the bridge and witnessing the Sea Hawk launch, fully realized what had happened, the catapult was up and ready to launch. Sea Hawks launched in fairly good sequence and fired at the towed target. Lt Cdr Gupta, the squadron commander, was so good that he shot off the towed

---

[1] A small box like structure on the flight deck of the *Vikrant* that housed the lights showing the state of the catapult. It was meant for the FDEO. The box looked like the 'howdah' on the back of an elephant in which the person taking a ride on the elephant sits. Hence, it's named 'howdah'.

target entirely on his first run of rocket firing. Later, the CNS remarked in jest that the Squadron CO was perhaps covering up the marksmanship of his other pilots.

The *Vikrant* had finally proved to the rest of the navy that even a limping ship could be put out to sea and perform her intended role, if the men behind the machines put their heart and soul in their job.

After the morning's shop window, the CNS went around the ship and came down to the forward engine room. He went straight to the boiler room and wanted to see the A1 boiler, now lying cold. Before heading back, he had a few words with H. Singh, petty officer mechanic engineering, who was controlling the A2 boiler. He asked about the welfare of his family back in Bombay: '*Ghar se chitthiya aatey hain* (Do letters come from home)?'

Prompt came the reply: '*Sir, haftey mey ek bar aatey hain* (Sir, they come once a week).'

The CNS engaged him more: '*Gharwali kya likhthi hain?* (What does your wife have to say)?'

The reply was spontaneous '*Sir, likhti hain, Dacca jaoge toh zaroor mulmul leke aana* (Sir, she writes that if you go to Dacca, then you must bring back muslin cloth).' The CNS got a whiff of the spirit down below and must have realized that this ship could win any war.

CNS Nanda was so happy after the visit that he granted permission for the ship to return for a quick visit to Bombay for Diwali. There was much merriment when this was announced and the sound production equipment operator quickly played '*Bombay meri hai*' on the main broadcast, right in the middle of the working hours. The trip to Bombay never happened, as we were diverted from Madras to Port Blair and thereafter to Port Cornwallis. That was a beautiful lagoon and there couldn't have been a better place to rest and recreate, before the balloon went up. The sailors of all departments on a warship are divided into three groups. Each group is on duty for four hours, while the other

two groups rest. The system is called three duty watch system.
The three duty watches take turn to cover a 12-hour period. The
system repeats after 12 hours, and works continuously.

When the *Vikrant* was anchored in the Andaman waters, the
officers and men from other departments who were off duty watch
took turns to go out and visit the islands for rest and recreation.
The personnel from the *Vikrant's* Engineering Department could
not be spared, as the ship was to sail at short notice and her
boilers and main engines were kept ready for her to weigh anchor
and set sail. The Engineering Department could not spare even
the off-duty watch personnel to leave the ship and go ashore to
visit the islands.

The Captain addressed the ship's company over the main
broadcast to let us know that for all purposes, we were at war.

After all the rigorous workup, the war itself became easy to
endure. Each time a sortie left the ship, there was that pregnant
eagerness for their safe return. A few Alizés got back with some
bullet holes. Apart from the official debriefing sessions, there was a
more light-hearted debrief for the ward room. Lt. Mohan Varghese
had some hilarious situations to narrate. The pilots were always
a bubbly lot and their enthusiasm always kept up our spirits.

We were blessed to have outstanding role models leading us
from the front. Capt. Parkash himself was an admirable man—a
man of very few words, but he was very clear in his intent
when he spoke. His address to the ship's company on the eve of
2 December was very clear and powerful. We knew we were at
war and there was no looking back. All heads of departments
were stalwarts and stood tall amongst us juniors: Cdr H.M.L.
Saxena as the executive officer was exceptionally good as a team
leader—he had an endearing way of getting things done. Cdr (E)
(later vice admiral) B.R. Chowdhury was a quiet man with clear
ideas and pragmatic vision. Senior Engineer Lt Cdr (later vice
admiral) Bharat Bhushan was an outstanding professional with
a cherubic smile and unending stock of Punjabi jokes to lighten

our hearts. Lt Cdr Suresh Soota, the FDEO, was as sharp as a knife. Shepherding us junior officers was Senior Watch Keeper Lt Kulwant Singh Bhasin, whose domineering spirit was dreaded by those who crossed his path. We had a bunch of very spirited sailors led by Master Chief Mechanic B.R. Sharma, a legend in his own right. Similarly, on the flight deck we had Chief E.R.A. Mathews, a bundle of energy. Then we had younger sailors, like Shaukeen Singh Yadav, Awasthi, Ratra, R.P. Singh, Vijay Sood, H.M. Sharma, A.K. Bhalla, Aurora, Nathan, and many others. Looking back, each one was a role model and we youngsters learnt from their collective experience. We were a happy lot and interacted with ease at all levels.

The war came to a rather abrupt end, when we had entered Paradip harbour for refuelling. We could have continued forever if there was a need. The FOC-in-C Admiral Krishnan flew back after participating in the surrender agreement signing event and addressed the ship's company, to give us a first-hand feel of what a stupendous victory the nation had won. There was much merrymaking on board and the trip back to Bombay was memorable, with heart-warming receptions at Paradip, Madras and Cochin.

The efforts of the Engine Room department were well recognized. The Commander (E) was awarded VrC, the senior engineer and the FDEO were awarded Nao Sena Medal, and the senior watchkeeper and a number of key sailors were awarded Mention in Despatches.

Rarely ever does an Engine Room department get a chance to prove their mettle so demonstratively. Very often, men who run the machines are taken for granted, and they seldom get any adulatory attention beyond the gangways of the ship. A limping *Vikrant* gave us a chance to show off our skills and bravery. It might be difficult for the current generation, used to better technology and touch type controls, to imagine what we went through in the mind-numbing heat of the engine rooms, with so many uncertainties of operating boilers, which could have burst at any moment. Those moments of danger and elation could only be felt and not described. So, today, when some youngster asks me what we did on the *Vikrant* during the war, I just reply, 'Oh. We put the screws on.'

Annexures

ROLL OF HONOUR

1971 War Gallantry Awards-INS Vikrant

Rank and Name	Award	Remarks
Capt. Swaraj Parkash	Maha Vir Chakra	Commanding Officer INS Vikrant
Cdr B.R. Chowdhury	Vir Chakra	Engineer Officer INS Vikrant
Cdr R.S. Grewal	Vir Chakra	Commander Air INS Vikrant
Cdr H.M.L. Saxena	Nao Sena Medal	Executive Officer INS Vikrant
Surg. Cdr G.P. Christian	Nao Sena Medal	Medical Officer INS Vikrant
Lt Cdr Bharat Bhushan	Nao Sena Medal	Senior Engineer Officer INS Vikrant
Lt Cdr Y.K. Satija	Nao Sena Medal	Air Engineer Officer INS Vikrant
Lt Cdr Suresh Soota	Nao Sena Medal	Flight Deck Engineer Officer INS Vikrant

Lt (SDR) Kashmira Singh	Nao Sena Medal	Assistant Electrical Officer INS Vikrant
Lt SD (B) Darshan Lal	Nao Sena Medal	INS Vikrant
T.V.R. Nambiar, MCPO II (AH)	Nao Sena Medal	Captain Flight Deck INS Vikrant
K.S. Salaria, MCPO (AH) II VSM	Nao Sena Medal	Hangar Control Chief INS Vikrant
R.P. Singh, Mech 3	Nao Sena Medal	INS Vikrant
C.S. Tyagi, PO (GI)	Nao Sena Medal	INS Vikrant
Lt P.B.S. Gujral	Mention in Despatches	INS Vikrant

1971 War Gallantry Awards-INAS 300

White Tigers Sea Hawk Squadron

Rank and Name	Award	Remarks
Lt Cdr Santosh Kumar Gupta	Maha Vir Chakra	Commanding Officer
Lt Cdr Ashwini Kumar Mehra	Vir Chakra	Pilot
Lt R.S. Sodhi	Vir Chakra	Pilot
Lt V.K. Datta	Vir Chakra	Pilot
Lt Prem Kumar	Vir Chakra	Pilot
Lt Gurnam Singh	Nao Sena Medal (Gal)	Squadron Air Engineer Officer
Lt Cdr G. Israni	Mention in Despatches	Pilot

Lt Cdr Ashok Sinha	Mention in Despatches	Pilot
Lt Cdr P.D. Sharma	Mention in Despatches	Pilot
Lt Cdr Y.M. Bhide	Mention in Despatches	Pilot
Lt R. Shahdadpuri	Mention in Despatches	Squadron Air Electrical Officer
V.R. Sampath Kumar, M. Ch. AA II	Mention in Despatches	Squadron Master Chief Aircraft Artificer

1971 War Gallantry Awards-INAS 310

Cobra Alize Squadron

Rank and Name	Award	Remarks
Lt Cdr R.D. Dhir	Vir Chakra	Commanding Officer
Lt Cdr S.P. Ghosh	Vir Chakra	Observer
Lt Cdr S. Ramsagar	Vir Chakra	Pilot
Lt Cdr Ashok Roy	Vir Chakra	Pilot (Posthumous)
Lt B.B. Bhagwat	Vir Chakra	Observer
Lt K.S. Panwar	Vir Chakra	Observer
Lt M.V. Paul	Nao Sena Medal (Gal)	Squadron Air Electrical Officer
M.K. Vijayan, MCPO (A/M)	Nao Sena Medal (Gal)	Posthumous
Lt Harbir Singh Sirohi	Mention in Despatches	Observer

CITATION FOR MAHAVIR CHAKRA

Captain Swaraj Parkash, AVSM (00022-Z)[1]

Captain Swaraj Parkash Commanded INS VIKRANT which was the nucleus of the Naval interdiction and strike force operating against the enemy in the Bay of Bengal. Throughout the period of these operations, the ship was operating in most hazardous waters and was the principal target both for enemy Submarines and Aircraft. With indomitable spirit, he launched ceaseless offensive operations against the enemy. The successful air strikes from the VIKRANT had devastating effect on Ports all along the Bangladesh coast and completely denied the enemy use of sea and inland waterways. The complete supremacy of our Naval force symbolized by the VIKRANT paralyzed the enemy, shattered his morale and considerably expedited the enemy's capitulation in the Eastern Theatre.

Captain Swaraj Parkash displayed conspicuous gallantry inspiring leadership, professional skill and devotion to duty in keeping with the highest traditions of the Indian Navy.

---

[1]'Captain Swaraj Parkash', *Gallantry Awards, Ministry of Defence, Government of India,* https://tinyurl.com/4kexnyap. Accessed on 10 October 2023.

CITATION FOR MAHAVIR CHAKRA

Lieutenant Commander Santosh Kumar
Gupta (NM 00311-F)
Effective Date of the Award
9th December 1971[2]

Lieutenant Commander Santosh Kumar Gupta, Commanding Officer of a Navy air squadron, operating from the air-craft carrier INS VIKRANT, led a total of eleven very successful strike missions with devastating effects on enemy ships and heavily defended shore facilities in various sectors of Bangladesh. On 9th December 1971, Lt Commander Gupta pressed home a strike of Seahawk aircraft against enemy targets in Khulna in face of a fierce barrage of anti-aircraft gun fire. His aircraft was hit and damaged by the enemy fire. However, regardless of his personal safety and in the face of extreme danger, Lt Commander Gupta continued to lead the attack with indomitable determination and skill and then led his divisions on board, back safely. Lt Commander Gupta showed great courage and professional ability in landing his damaged aircraft safely on board the carrier. On the remaining missions, Lt Commander Gupta on all occasions successfully led his squadron to attack harbour and shore installations and against enemy shipping with crippling effect, in spite of heavy ground oppositions. This eventually assisted in the successful termination of resistance from the enemy in Chalna, Khulna and Chitiagong area.

Throughout the operations, Lt Commander Gupta displayed conspicuous gallantry and outstanding leadership.

---

[2]'Rear Admiral (Then, Lieutenant Commander) Santosh Kumar Gupta', *Gallantry Awards, Ministry of Defence, Government of India*, https://tinyurl.com/mr2cp4hk. Accessed on 10 October 2023.

INSTRUMENT OF SURRENDER

The PAKISTAN Eastern Command agree to surrender all PAKISTAN Armed Forces in BANGLA DESH to Lieutenant-General JAGJIT SINGH AURORA, General Officer Commanding in Chief of the Indian and BANGLA DESH forces in the Eastern Theatre. This surrender includes all PAKISTAN land, air and naval forces as also all para-military forces and civil armed forces. These forces will lay down their arms and surrender at the places where they are currently located to the nearest regular troops under the command of Lieutenant-General JAGJIT SINGH AURORA.

The PAKISTAN Eastern Command shall come under the orders of Lieutenant-General JAGJIT SINGH AURORA as soon as this instrument has been signed. Disobedience of orders will be regarded as a breach of the surrender terms and will be dealt with in accordance with the accepted laws and usages of war. The decision of Lieutenant-General JAGJIT SINGH AURORA will be final, should any doubt arise as to the meaning or interpretation of the surrender terms.

Lieutenant-General JAGJIT SINGH AURORA gives a solemn assurance that personnel who surrender shall be treated with dignity and respect that soldiers are entitled to in accordance with the provisions of the GENEVA Convention and guarantees the safety and well-being of all PAKISTAN military and para-military forces who surrender. Protection will be provided to foreign nationals, ethnic minorities and personnel of WEST PAKISTAN origin by the forces under the command of Lieutenant-General JAGJIT SINGH AURORA.

(JAGJIT SINGH AURORA)
Lieutenant-General
General Officer Commanding in Chief
Indian and BANGLA DESH Forces in the
Eastern Theatre
16 December 1971.

(AMIR ABDULLAH KHAN NIAZI)
Lieutenant-General
Martial Law Administrator Zone B and
Commander Eastern Command (PAKISTAN)
16 December 1971.

PRIME MINISTER

No.312-PMH/71   New Delhi,
                                December 22, 1971.

Dear Admiral Nanda,

          The Navy's exploits in these fourteen
days of fighting will long be remembered. The
achievements of our Naval Forces have thrilled
the nation. Your leadership and the daring
and the skill of our Fleet have made singular
contribution to the success of the war on both
fronts. I should like to express the gratitude
of the Government and the people of India to
you and to your officers and men.

          None of this would have been possible
without the most exacting leadership and
dedication at all levels. In this, your role
has been crucial. No words can be a better
recompense for your labours than the people's
admiration and India's success.

          With kindest regards,

                         Yours sincerely,

                         (Indira Gandhi)

Admiral S.M.Nanda,
Chief of the Naval Staff,
New Delhi.

Nanda, S.M., *The Man Who Bombed Karachi: A Memoir*, HarperCollins
Publishers India, 2004.

ADMIRAL S. M. NANDA, PVSM
CHIEF OF THE NAVAL STAFF

NAVAL HEADQUARTERS
NEW DELHI - 11

27th December, 1971.

My dear Prime Minister,

    I am most grateful for your kind letter and your generous tribute to the Navy's contribution during the recent conflict with Pakistan.

    It is a matter of pride to a fighting Service to carry out its tasks in a fitting manner, and no reward could be greater for the Navy than to receive the gratitude and admiration of their countrymen.

    Our task has been easier because our men were motivated by the justness of our cause and sustained by the solidarity of the country under your inspiring leadership.

    On behalf of all officers and sailors in the Navy, I would like to assure you that we remain ready to meet any challenge to the integrity of our country.

With kind regards,

Yours sincerely,

Shrimati INDIRA GANDHI,
Prime Minister,
1, Safdarjung Road,
NEW DELHI.

Adm Nanda's letter of thanks to Prime Minister - 27 Dec 1971

Ibid.

Acknowledgements

We wish to acknowledge the help received as we made progress on this book. We would like to mention in particular Commodore Lalit Shanker (Retd), Dr Harmanmohan Singh Sandhu and Cdr Arun Saigal (Retd) for their guidance in locating sources for the authentic information that we needed. We thank Shri Singh, advocate, Delhi High Court; Ronjaboti Sen, advocate, Calcutta High Court; Reeta Gooptu Sen and Jyoti Kaur in ordering and arranging the books we needed for referencing. They also read the manuscript from time to time, and gave their valuable suggestions from the readers' point of view.

We remember Seetha Gupta, wife of Rear Admiral S.K. Gupta, who was a force behind this book but unfortunately died a year before the book could see the light of the day. We thank Varsha Gupta, their daughter who has been an inspiration for the book after her mother's departure.

There are many others to who we turned time and again to confirm names, dates and the sequence of events, which to our minds were significant for the reportage of events that took place over half a century earlier. We are unable to mention each one of them individually, but we are very grateful to them.

Bibliography

Ahluwalia (Retd), Lieutenant Commander Madanjit Singh, *Torpedoed at Sea: The Saga of INS Khukri*, Notion Press, 2016.

Bhutto, Fatima, *Songs of Blood and Sword: A Daughter's Memoir*, Penguin India, 2011.

Hiranandani, G.M., *Transition to Triumph: History of the Indian Navy, 1965-1975*; Spantech & Lancer, 2000.

Krishnan, N., *No Way But Surrender: An Account of Vice Admiral N Krishnan Indo-Pakistan War in the Bay of Bengal, 1971*, Vikas Publishing House, 1980.

Mohanan, Kalesh, *The Royal Indian Navy; Trajectories, Transformations and the Transfer of Power*, Routledge India, 2021.

Nanda, S.M., *The Man Who Bombed Karachi: A Memoir*, HarperCollins Publishers India, 2004.

Panikkar, K.M., *India and the Indian Ocean: An Essay on the influence of Sea Power on Indian History*.

Pasricha, Vinod, *Downwind, Four Green*, Pashmira Publications, 2010.

Prasad, S.N., and U.P. Thapliyal, *The India-Pakistan War of 1971: A History*, Natraj Publishers, 2019.

Roy, Mihir K., *War in the Indian Ocean*, Spantech & Lancer, 1995.

Singh, Satyendra, *Under Two Ensigns: The Indian Navy, 1945–1950*, Oxford & IBH Publishing, 1986.

Tharoor, Shashi, *An Era of Darkness: The British Empire in India*, Aleph, 2016.

Index